GHOST WALKS IN
DERBYSHIRE
AND THE PEAK DISTRICT

GHOST WALKS
IN DERBYSHIRE

AND THE PEAK DISTRICT

Barbara Wadd

First published in Great Britain in 2001 by
The Breedon Books Publishing Company Limited
Breedon House, 3 The Parker Centre, Derby, DE21 4SZ.

This edition published in Great Britain in 2012 by The Derby Books
Publishing Company Limited, 3 The Parker Centre, Derby, DE21 4SZ.

ISBN 978-1-78091-190-8

Printed and bound by Copytech (UK) Limited, Peterborough.

Index of Walks

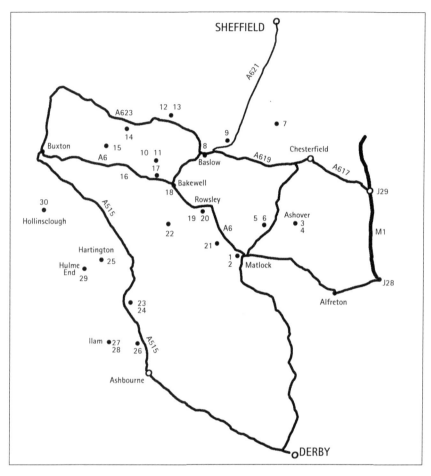

Acknowledgements

I wish to acknowledge the contribution made to this book by my friends, Sue Broadrick, Margaret Moore and Roy Perkins.

Sue and Margaret, laboured as my chief 'walk checkers' deciphering my instructions, and Roy, who contributed walks, kept an eye on my map reading and many times set me on the right path.

You encouraged me to write it, stuck with me through over 400 miles of walking, through rain, shine and mud (who will ever forget Musden Wood!) and made the whole enterprise great fun and enjoyable.

I couldn't have done it without you.

Introduction

THIS is a collection of 30 circular walks set in Derbyshire and the Peak District, the walks ranging from 2-10 miles in length. Each walk has at least one ghostly story attached to a part of it, some walks having several chilling tales, which hopefully, will bring a shiver to even the most warmly clad rambler! The stories include lanes where you may encounter phantom coaches, headless horsemen, ghostly dogs which haunt crossroads foretelling death, the eerie sounds of a 500-year-old murder, haunted mines, pubs and houses and even a funeral cortège of 12 headless men!

The walks cover a wide range of Derbyshire scenery, allowing you to enjoy the gentle delights of fields, woods and valleys, the open views of the harsher gritstone edges and the dramatic beauty of limestone country, with a spectacular ascent of Chrome Hill in the Upper Dove Valley.

As well as the ghostly tales, some of the walks follow ancient packhorse trails and saltways, the evidence of which you may see in guideposts, bridges and paving and you will find information regarding this fascinating mode of transport scattered throughout the walks for additional interest. Other stories include folktales, explanations of strange place names or quaint houses, information about some of the mines which abound in the Derbyshire countryside, including a Bronze Age copper mine and any other unusual features, such as a set of stocks, a bull ring and an ancient yew tree.

Each walk has an introductory description, telling you the area covered, the type of terrain and highlighting its best attributes. Your attention is drawn to special features, such as a recommended time of year for doing the walk – e.g. May time – because the woods are full of bluebells and wild garlic or when well dressings take place in certain villages.

The distance of each walk is given in miles and the walks are graded from A to D i.e. from Easy to Demanding, with an explanation of the grades being provided at the front of the book.

Information is given regarding parking at the start of the walk, together with directions where thought necessary and a map grid reference is also stated.

There is a suggested pub stop for you to have liquid refreshment on all but the shortest walks. On the longer walks, this is reached at approximately the mid-point to coincide with a lunch break. Where the pub is not reached until later, you are given warning at the start.

WC facilities are identified where available, both at the start of walks, en route and of course, the pub provides a mid-point comfort stop.

My friends and I have walked over 400 miles to put these walks together, compiling the routes and checking that the instructions are correct and as unambiguous as possible. Therefore, the walk directions are very detailed and hopefully, clear, and the text has been broken into numbered sections, which relate to a sketch map. The sketch map also shows features such as farms, woods, roads and other points, which should assist you in navigation.

'Confirmers', i.e. points that tell you that you are on the right path, are included throughout the instructions, and some, such as the name of a lane, or farm, may be checked against an Ordnance Survey map if carried.

If the instructions do not seem to match the terrain, stop and think for a moment. If necessary, retrace your steps to the last point where they fitted, rather than continuing and trying to make them fit.

A map is not essential for the walks, but information is given as to which Ordnance Survey map may be used. You may find one useful as an aid to navigation or in case you have to divert from the planned route due to, for example, flooding. It is also an easy way to get used to map reading, by checking the walk instructions against a map and seeing how the information fits.

It has been my intention to produce a book which will be useful and interesting, intriguing and amusing and one which, whilst showing you the delights of the Derbyshire countryside, will also give you a taste of its rich folk history.

I hope that you will enjoy using it as much as I have enjoyed compiling it.

Note: Some details will necessarily have been duplicated as some walks cover the same areas and overlap the same stories.

Degree of Difficulty

The walks are graded as follows, taking into account ascents, descents, terrain underfoot and length of walks. Grading may span two categories.

A. Easy: Gently undulating terrain. Taking into account the mileage, it should be well within the capabilities of regular walkers and fit occasional walkers.

B. Moderate: One or two longer or steeper ascents/descents but suitable for regular walkers who can manage the distance.

C. Energetic: Steeper ascents/descents, distance and rougher terrain making it a more demanding walk. Should be within the capabilities of reasonably experienced regular walkers.

D. Demanding: For fit and experienced walkers only. Steep ascents/ descents and difficult terrain.

Equipment

Walking boots are recommended for all the walks. In view of the mileage they will make even the walks graded 'A' Easy, more enjoyable. In dry summer weather, lightweight boots would be suitable for A and B grades.

Suitable outerwear, including waterproof coats and trousers, hats and gloves should be taken.

Other equipment recommended:

Food and drink: At least some emergency rations, e.g.chocolate for quick energy boost. Also take plenty of water in summer to avoid dehydration and a hot drink in winter.

Compass.

Whistle: For emergency use only.

Torch (and spare batteries): In case you misjudge the time and night falls.

Survival Bag or Space Blanket: Useful in case of accident to wrap casualty to keep them warm.

Rucksack: Leaves hands free.

First Aid kit: Plasters and blister kit, antiseptic cream.

Maps: Not essential as detailed instructions and a sketch map are provided. However, a map is useful as a back-up in case of confusion or in the event of diversion from the walk route due to adverse conditions e.g. flooding.

Information on sketch maps

FB   Footbridge

......   Route follows footpath, other footpath.

----   Route follows track, other track.

——   Route follows road or lane, other road/lane

Other Terms used in text:

Green Lane – wide path, often grassy, between walls.

Heading diagonally across field.

Bearing right, bearing left.

Bear right to 2 o'clock.
Bear left to 10 o'clock.

Turn through 180°.

Walk 1
Matlock – Winster

A varied walk, which starts with a steady climb, giving good views back over Matlock. The first half of the walk is mainly on the Limestone Way, to Bonsall and on to the village of Winster, which was mentioned in *Domesday Book* and is full of historical and ghostly interest. It then takes in Clough Wood and Cambridge Wood and the attractive wide grassy valley in Wensley Dale, finishing with a walk by the River Derwent.

Distance: 10 miles.
Grade: B.
Parking: Matlock Railway Station car park. Off A6 by Matlock Bridge. Go past pay-and-display car park to the public car park at the back which is free.
Map Ref: SK295604. Outdoor Leisure 24 White Peak Area.
Pub Stop: Miners' Standard pub, Winster.

Bonsall takes part in the well dressings each year. Three wells are dressed, plus children's wells and takes place in Carnival Week, usually the last Saturday in July.

Route
1. Come out of the car park back to the road and turn right and immediately right again, up the road with the Bank of Scotland on the corner. A short distance further on, turn left on to the footpath marked 'Limestone Way'. The path climbs quite steeply emerging into open fields, where you keep straight ahead. Cross a track and go straight over into a wooded area. After the wooded area, go through an open gateway and then follow hedge on the left for four fields, then go through another open gateway into fifth field and

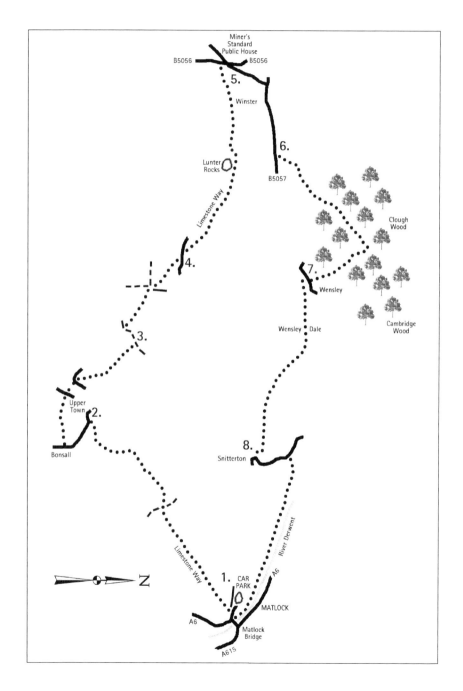

straight on to a stile in the corner. Continue up next field, going to the right of Masson Lees Farm.

Cross stile over a track and over the stile ahead, bearing right up the hill to reach another track. Turn right on this track and then left on to a footpath a short distance along it. Continue up the slope (the last bit of climbing on this part of the walk!) and then go over the stile to your right. Then bear left across the corner of the field. Go over the stile and straight across a stony lane. Continue ahead on a path across three fields. This path then joins a wider path, where you turn left and start to descend. Where the path forks, take the right fork, continuing down until you reach a stile by a gate. Cross over to another stile and continue, to emerge on a lane by some cottages, eventually reaching the road. This is a convenient spot for a coffee break.

2. Turn left down the road and continue until you reach the stone cross in the centre of Bonsall. Turn right here on to a footpath (marked Limestone Way) by the side of a cottage, climbing up a series of steps on to a stony path between walls and keeping straight ahead to the road in Uppertown. Turn left and immediately right and continue along this road to a junction. Bear right on to the footpath on the corner of the two roads and go straight ahead across three fields, then, crossing into the fourth field, follow the wall on your left for five fields, then continue straight ahead until you reach a track.

3. Turn left on the track and a short distance further on, look for a footpath on the right-hand side. Turn right here and follow path across six more fields to a lane. Turn right on this lane and then at another lane on your left, go over the stile on the right-hand corner. Continue across next fields to a road.

4. Turn left and then right back on to the footpath. Cross first field diagonally to the corner, then four more fields until a view opens up of Wensley Dale below and you follow a wall on your right. On reaching a stile, cross over the wall and continue to the left until you reach some trees on your left and a stone outcrop known as Lunter Rocks. (A pleasant place for a picnic lunch before your pub stop!). Just after the rocks, cross a stile and bear left up the hill diagonally to the corner of the field, to a stone gateway to join a track, where you turn right. Continue on this track until you reach

the road. Turn right down the road and left at the junction to reach the Miners' Standard pub, on the outskirts of Winster.

5. Coming out of the pub, cross the road and continue across to the minor road, where you turn left, going down through Winster to the main road (B5057) at the bottom. Turn right here, and pause to note some points of interest.

On the opposite side of the road there is Winster Hall, a three storey house with a parapet at the top. Here, it is said that in the 18th century, the daughter of the house and the coachman fell in love but her parents, objecting to the match arranged a 'better' marriage for her. The night before the wedding, the daughter and the coachman climbed to the top of the building, swore to love each other forever, and jumped to their deaths. It is said that near Christmastime each year, the ghostly lovers repeat their fatal leap. They are buried opposite the door of Winster Church. The courtyard is said to be haunted by the ghost of the tragic daughter and locked doors within the hall are found to be unaccountably opened.

Winster Hall, where two tragic lovers jumped from the parapet to their deaths.

The (former) Angel Inn, with three storeys, gable end; a coaching inn of dubious reputation and to the right, the Market Hall, Winster.

As you continue along the road, on the right-hand side there is the Market Hall, a 16th-century building, where the upper floor is thought to have been originally timber framed. It was the first property the National Trust acquired in Derbyshire and is now a National Trust Information Centre. A ghostly hooded figure has been seen kneeling on the pavement in front of the Market Hall.

On the opposite side of the road from the Market Hall is the former Angel Inn (three storeys with gable end and an arched gateway). This was a former coaching inn of dubious reputation. The building is full of stories of doors opening and closing on their own and sounds of footsteps. A murder is said to have been committed in one of the bedrooms there and a woman staying in it, was woken by ghostly hands gripping her throat.

In another story, a woman, sitting before a mirror in a bedroom on the first floor, saw a figure in a bridal dress coming down the stairs from the floor above. However, when the figure entered the room and was seen to be headless, the poor woman fainted.

Continue along this road until you reach the end of the houses, past the school on your right, then turn left at the footpath sign on your left.

6. The path bears right down the fields, and continues in the same direction until it finally reaches the edge of the wood. Go over the stile here and into Clough Wood. Continue through this pleasant wooded area for about a mile, until you reach a stony track crossing your own. Turn right and immediately right again, then left to footpath sign and go over a wooden bridge. Go straight ahead, then left at arrow sign, to head up into Cambridge Wood. This is a short but fairly stiff climb. When you leave the wood, keep straight ahead across the fields to the road at Wensley.

7. Turn right at the road and then left on a footpath going through a gap in the wall. The path bears round left and then, where the track can be seen rising ahead and there is another track to the right, go between these two tracks, on a broad grassy path, down the valley of Wensley Dale. As you are leaving the broad grassy area and you see a small building ahead, the footpath goes to the right along the lane. (There is a sign 'Footpath to Matlock' marked in such big letters on the wall that you miss it!). The path crosses back into the fields and continues straight ahead for about ¾ mile. Pass the first buildings on your right, but then head diagonally right to the corner, where you will find a narrow path between the buildings, taking you to the road in Snitterton.

On a triangle of grass in front of the post box, note the bullring. This was used in the barbaric practice bull baiting, where a bull was tied to the ring and baited by dogs. It was thought to make the meat more tender.

8. Turn left on the road, and on the second left-hand bend, after a sign for 'Oker' (Oaker on some maps) and passing Brookdale House on your right, take the footpath to the right. Stay on this path, which joins the River Derwent and with the river on your left, continue all the way back to the car park, which is on your right. Turn right here back to the main car park.

Walk 2
Matlock –
Cocking Tor

A fairly easy walk, in undulating countryside, with good views over the Amber Valley from Cocking Tor. It includes a wishing stone and, later in the walk, visits Riber Castle, haunted by a blue lady and a military figure.

Distance: 8½ miles.

Grade: A.

Parking: Start from Matlock Railway Station, entrance off A6 by Matlock Bridge. Pass the pay-and-display car park at the front and park in the back car park, which is free.

Map Ref: SK295604. Outdoor Leisure 24 White Peak Area.

Pub Stop: The Gate pub at Tansley Knoll, two-thirds of way round walk, too late for lunch.

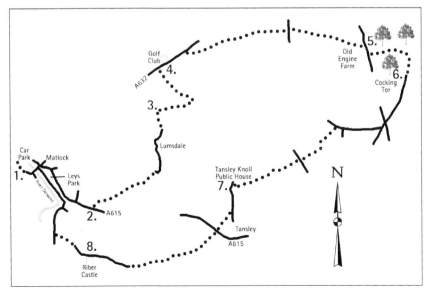

Route

1. Go out of car park and turn left over the bridge over the River Derwent. On far side of bridge, cross the road at the lights and bear left then right into the park, going to the left of the clock. Keep on path on the left-hand edge of the park, parallel to the road (A615 Alfreton/Tansley Road) until you pass through the children's play area.

Leave the park at this point, going on to the road and continuing straight ahead. Riber Castle may be seen on the hill ahead. At the next set of traffic lights, cross over and continue on the left side of the road. A short distance further on, turn left on a footpath behind the Scout headquarters, on the right-hand corner of Butts Drive.

2. Follow this footpath to the road in Lumsdale. Turn left on the road, which then winds left and right through old mills, passing a glass blowing studio (unfortunately closed Saturday/Sunday). You then reach a footpath to both the right and the left. The left-hand path leads up to the Wishing Stone. It is quite a steep climb over uneven steps, which have been worn away by the many visitors over the years. However, the climb is worth it if only for the view from the top.

The Wishing Stone is a huge slab of millstone grit, in which is thought to dwell a nature spirit, which was much visited in Victorian times. To have your wish granted, you simply walk around it three times, whilst repeating your wish under your breath. Provided you do not wish for money or material gain, your wish may be granted within three cycles of the moon.

After visiting the stone, return to the road below and turn left. After two more S bends, right and left, go up a footpath, in the wall on the right-hand side, through a small wood on to a stony track bearing right. Go over the stile and to the left to the Reservoir, which is a good place for a coffee stop.

Return to the lane on your left and go straight ahead past the cottages on your right. Then just before the house on your left, take the footpath to your right, crossing the stream at the stepping stones.

3. Go up the track and where the wall goes to the right, keep straight

ahead into the wood. Stay on the main track, which sweeps right and then in a long sweep to the left. Where the path straightens and you see a rocky outcrop on the hillock ahead, take a left fork on a rising path and keep straight ahead until you leave the trees. Turn left on a grassy track, which then curves right. Keep straight ahead on this track, passing a quarry on your right, back into trees and gradually dropping down to a main road (A632).

4. Turn right on the road, past a golf club and then turn right at a footpath sign and cross a field, keeping a building on your right. Cross a wall and turn left up the path to another wall. Go through a stile. Continue in the same direction, crossing two more fields to the road. Cross the road and follow track opposite through a wooded area, then across two fields, then back into a wooded area. Then go across three more fields to a road. Cross this road and continue straight ahead, going down the fields and up the other side. Go along the top of next field, with a wall on your left, then go left, passing to the left of the water, through a stile, then up the hill, going to the left of Old Engine Farm to the road.

Old Engine Farm was named for the pumping engine, which pumped the water from the Gregory Mine, which was below Cocking Tor.

5. Turn right on the road, passing the farm with its old millstones, then turn left on to a track, heading towards a copse. Go to the right side of the copse (not into it), then two thirds of the way round, take footpath to the right across the field. Turn left along wall to next wood.

Cross stile in corner, go down path and then to the right (may be slippery in wet weather). Keep to the higher path and ignore a path dropping down left. Continue, passing small outcrops of rock until you reach a large flat slab of rock, which is Cocking Tor.

This is a good viewpoint, with views of the Amber Valley, with Ogston Reservoir to be seen ahead and the village of Ashover to be seen to the left. Spare some time also, to read the graffiti, carved in this rock, which has been a meeting point for lovers for many, many years it seems!

6. Continue in the same direction and take the steep path leading down from Cocking Tor – very steep in places, so take your time and go carefully.

Where the path forks near the bottom, take the path to the right towards a wall and a building, going on to a track. Turn right on this track and go up the hill. On reaching a road, go straight on, then turn first right.

After passing a track to the left, turn left on to a footpath and cross three fields, then go through a wooded area and another field to the road. Go straight over road and down three fields. At a wood, bear left then down three more fields to a track. Go down the track to the road and turn right to The Gate pub in Tansley Knoll.

7. Go down the village on the main road, passing the church and then take footpath to the right. Following the hedge on the left-hand side, go down the field to a bridge across a stream and up to the road at Tansley.

Cross the road on to the track, which is to the right of the private drive opposite and turn immediately left on the footpath. Go straight up following wall. On reaching a field, go straight ahead, keeping wall on the right for two fields. Crossing into next field, continue now keeping wall on

Riber Castle, built by John Smedley in 1862; it is said to be haunted by two ghosts.

the left across four more fields, heading towards Riber Castle to be seen ahead. In the fourth field look for the footpath sign on the left. Cross the wall here, then bear right to a stile by a gate. Go over the stile and straight ahead, crossing fields to the track. Turn right on the track and then left at the road. Then continue straight ahead up the hill, turning on to the footpath to the right of the gates of the castle. Go down this narrow path, which opens out to a view of Matlock below.

John Smedley, a local mill owner, built this Gothic fake, known as Riber Castle in 1862. He was one of the developers of Matlock as a spa town and his 'Hydro' brought him great wealth. Riber Castle is said to be the haunt of two ghosts, a figure in military uniform, who marches through the walls of the castle and a blue lady, who wanders through the corridors and rooms.

8. Go down steep path to a road, where you turn right. Just past the church, turn left down a steep road. Turn left at the bottom and go straight through the park to the bridge. Turn left over the bridge and on the other side, turn right back to car park.

Walk 3
Ashover 1

An easy but pleasant walk from the village of Ashover, across the fields and lanes. A headless woman, a haunted coffin, and a smoking ghost all add to the interest.

Distance: 2½ miles.
Grade: A.
Parking: Village Hall car park, Ashover. From B6036, turn up Church Street, past the church, following sign for car park. Continue past Crispin Inn, then bear right at Black Swan pub, following sign for car park and Alton. The car park is on the right, just past next bend.
Map Ref: SK351633. Ordnance Survey Pathfinder 761, Chesterfield.
Pub Stop: Crispin Inn or Black Swan pub, in Ashover.

Route

1. Turn left out of the car park and go down the road, bearing left at the junction down Church Street to the church.

There is a record of there being a church at Ashover in *Domesday Book*.

A headless woman is said to haunt the churchyard, last officially recorded as being seen in 1890, when spotted in the north aisle of the church at 8pm by a local. The ghost is said to be the wife of a farmer, John Townrow, who in 1841 bludgeoned her to death before cutting off her head and then slitting his own throat.

Some years before this last apparition, in 1879, a skull was found by a workman at Stubben Edge Hall, which is south of Ashover. One theory is that the skull was removed from Ashover churchyard for a wager and taken to the hall and the headless spectre is therefore searching for her head.

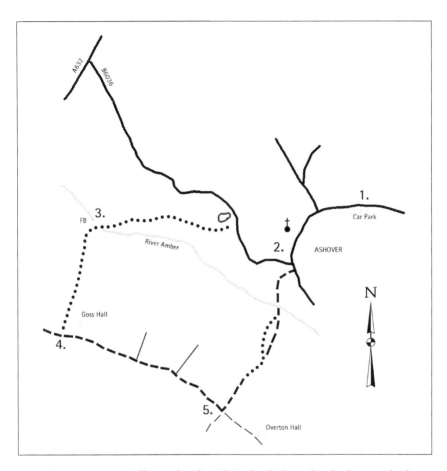

An empty stone coffin in the church is also believed to be haunted. If you walk round the empty coffin three times, then lie within it with your eyes closed, it is said you will then hear the ghostly sounds of rattling chains, faintly at first and then more loudly.

2. Continue to the T-junction at the bottom and turn right. Pass a footpath on the left and then, just before some houses, go left on an unmarked lane and ahead between walls to reach a stile. Go over the stile and bear right, dropping down the field. Go to the right at the bottom, finally reaching a stile and stone bridge, a wooden bridge and another stile,

with a choice of directions. Go straight on, on a wide track, passing a sign for a private quarry on the left. Then cross two tracks, and look for a stone bridge on the left over a stream (River Amber).

3. Turn left here over the bridge and go up the field with a wall/hedge on your left. Continue in the same direction, crossing the next field going through open gateways into the third and fourth fields, now with the hedge/wall on your right.

The house to the left ahead is Goss Hall, which dates back to the 16th century. Built in the reign of Elizabeth I, it is said to have belonged to Sir Walter Raleigh for a brief period. It is reputed to have a ghost that smoked a pipe, which filled the house with tobacco smoke. It was apparently so bad in the 1950s that it caused one owner to leave. Is there some connection between the pipe smoking ghost and Sir Walter Raleigh who introduced tobacco to this country?

Go through two stiles and over the fifth and last field to reach a lane.

4. Turn left on the lane. Pass a footpath to the left, then a footpath to the right and a track to the left. Continue following the public footpath sign directing you along the lane until you reach a crossroads of tracks.

Looking straight ahead and slightly left you can see the 16th-century Overton Hall. In 1887, 26 skeletons were discovered when work was being done in the grounds to create a tennis court. They appeared to have been buried hastily, perhaps as the result of plague. Coins found 30 yards away were dated 1742.

In the 1950s, the wife of a Pentecostal pastor refused to live at the hall because she said it was haunted.

The figure of a woman is said to haunt the grassy forecourt. She is thought to be the third wife of one of the Jessops who occupied the hall.

5. Turn left at the crossroads. Go up the track, then at next junction go ahead on to the footpath down field (which appears to be an old packhorse trail) continuing down to a bridge over the River Amber. Climb up the track, turning left at the road, then immediately right at junction, up the road past the church, continuing until you reach the car park.

Walk 4
Ashover 2

This is an undulating walk from the village of Ashover, through a variety of fields and woods. It has pleasant open views and reaches the attractive Ogston Reservoir in time for lunch. Its return via Ravensnest Tor gives superb views of the Amber Valley.

Ashover has an unusual folk tale, in the character of Dorothy Matley. The walk also goes through Handley, a village which was the scene of ghostly sightings and passes the haunted Overton Hall, where 26 skeletons were found.

Distance:	10 miles.
Grade:	B.
Parking:	Village Hall car park, Ashover. From B6036, turn up Church Street, past the church, following sign for car park. Continue past the Crispin Inn, then bear right at Black Swan pub, following sign for car park and Alton. The car park is on the right just past next bend.
Map Ref:	SK351633. Ordnance Survey Pathfinder 761, Chesterfield.
Pub Stop:	The New Napoleon, Ogston Reservoir.

In the 17th century, a character called Dorothy Matley lived in Ashover. She worked in a lead mine and was a great one for cursing and swearing. If accused of any misdeeds, she would protest her innocence, asking God to make the earth open up and swallow her if she were guilty. One day a young man accused her of stealing two penny pieces from him. Dorothy denied the theft in her usual strong language and then suddenly, according to the story, was seen to be spinning round, sinking further and further into the ground, until she was completely buried. When her lifeless body was finally

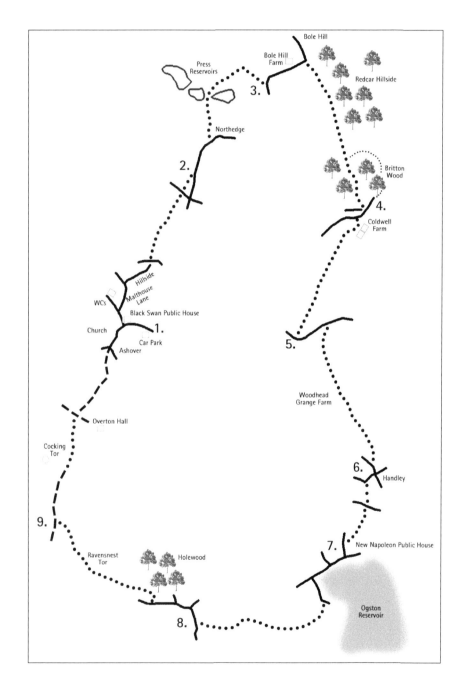

dug out, from about 12 feet down, two penny pieces were found in her pocket. Just another folktale? The parish register for deaths in 1660 shows Dorothy Matley forswore herself whereupon the ground opened and she sank over. Buried 2 March!

Route

1. Turn left out of car park, then, just after the Black Swan pub, take first turn right (signposted Toilets and Kelstedge, Matlock and Chesterfield). Then turn right up Malthouse Lane. (N.B. There are WCs just after the turn to Malthouse Lane, beyond phone box). After left-hand bend, turn right up Hillside, signposted Alton and Wingerworth. After the end of the cottages, look for a step stile in the stone wall on the left. Go up here through gorse and scrubland, over the stile at top and cross lane into the field. (There are good views looking back over Ashover and across to Cocking Tor). Continue with wall on the right for two fields then crossing into next field, continue with wall/hedge on the left for three more fields. Cross lane, then in next field cross diagonally to corner (not gate) to the stile and road.

2. Turn left on road and continue to the lane and farm on the left. Turn left here then bear right, to the stile by wooden gate, then bear slightly right through gateway and then diagonally right to bottom corner of field. Continue ahead, crossing between the two right-hand reservoirs. Then on reaching field, bear diagonally right to top corner, to a point midway between the two nearer buildings to be seen, dropping down into a scrubby area, then ahead through brambles and trees. Cross next field in same direction and then turn right on the track to the road.

3. Turn left on road, passing Bole Hill Farm and continuing up the hill. At the top take the **second** footpath right into wood. This is a pleasant place for a coffee stop. Continue straight ahead through wood and then where the paths divide near edge of wood, go right to a stile hidden in the corner, by side of wire fencing and leave the wood. There are good views to both sides at this point. Continue following wall/hedge on the right across three fields (ignoring two stiles on the right-hand side) to Britton Wood. Bear left downhill through wood, keeping to main path, ignoring path on the left-hand side, and continuing to the road.

4. Turn left, then immediately right on main road, following sign for Littlemoor and Ashover, then left on the track, which, after a short distance, bends right and left up the hill. At farm go straight on following the blue footpath sign, then turn right up the field and left at top on to the track. Then straight ahead, with holly hedge on the right, across the fields past another wooded area and continuing until you reach the road.

5. Turn left on road and go down the hill but look for an open gateway on the right where you turn on to a muddy track bearing round to the right to 2 o'clock. Continue across five fields. On reaching Woodhead Grange Farm, go to the left of the farm and then just before hedge turn right up railed wooden steps and then to the left, continuing along the right of the hedge for two fields, then go slightly right in third. Cross to two bar wooden stile in fourth, then following a hedge on the left in the fifth. In the sixth field, do not head for the gateway ahead, but go diagonally right to the top corner to the road and turn left.

6. Turn right at crossroads (in Handley) following sign for Woolley Moor and Ogston.

This pleasant village was the scene of a sighting, by four young ladies in a car, of a headless ghost on 14 March at about 8.20pm (no year given). It was said to be quite small, about the size of a child and dressed in an off-white smock. There was only the outline of a head and it was waving its arms about disjointedly. The occupants panicked at that point and drove off and though they later returned, saw nothing further. They did learn however, of another sighting of the ghost at almost the same place.

Crossroads seem to be a favourite haunt of ghosts and there are a number of theories as to why this should be. In the past, murderers and suicides were buried at crossroads, so perhaps their spirits are particularly restless. Also, witches were believed to practise black magic at crossroads and in doing so may have conjured up some strange apparitions!

Now turn left at the footpath. Facing the water, head diagonally right down field to bottom corner and cutting across corner of next field to the stile and road. Go straight over road on to the track. Bear slightly left at buildings, over the stile. Bear slightly right in field, then across corner of next field, continuing in same direction in last one to corner of field to reach the road.

7. Turn left down the road to the New Napoleon pub, overlooking Ogston Reservoir. Coming out of the pub, turn right and continue along road, crossing an arm of the reservoir, then turning first left. After right-hand bend, just past next building (Woolley Methodist Chapel which dates back to 1841), turn right on to the footpath, going along wall on the right-hand side and then bearing right up the field to top corner. Turn right on path then left over the stile by an iron gate. Turn right at next footpath arrow sign straight across middle of field. Continue straight ahead where paths cross at end of second field at edge of wood. Follow direction of arrow, on a well marked path, over two more fields, then in the next, bear left, following the direction of the finger post, picking up small marker post in field. Over two more stiles on to a track, between stone walls, over another stile and then to the left of the barn. Continue through the buildings of Clattercotes Farm, bearing left to the road.

8. Turn right on road, then left at next junction, following sign for Tansley and Matlock. Continue ahead (ignoring sign to the right for Ashover – you've more walking to do yet!) and up the hill and turn right at the footpath sign near top of hill, into Hole Wood. Climb up path through trees and then follow hedge on the left. Then bearing right following wall on the left, the path continues climbing quite steeply, but there are excellent views to the right of the Amber Valley to distract you, if you pause to catch your breath. (Ignore stile in the wall on the left near top). Continue ahead back into trees, then walking on the left-hand edge of trees until you finally reach a large stone trough. Turn left here up to a stile leading on to a track. The large rocky outcrop to the right is Cocking Tor, with Ashover in the distance in the valley.

9. Turn right down the track, passing below Cocking Tor, and then ahead on a path rising and falling through the spoil heaps of the old Gregory Mine, continuing straight ahead on a tree lined track, eventually dropping down and reaching a crossroads.

Overton Hall, where 26 skeletons were found in the grounds.

To the right is Overton Hall. In 1887, 26 skeletons were discovered when work was being done in the grounds to create a tennis court. They appeared to have been buried hastily, perhaps as the result of plague. Coins found nearby were dated 1742.

In the 1950s, the wife of a Pentecostal pastor refused to live at the hall because she said it was haunted.

The figure of a woman is said to haunt the grassy forecourt. She is thought to be the third wife of one of the Jessops who occupied the hall.

Your way continues straight over the crossroads. Then at next junction go ahead on to the footpath down field (which appears to be an old packhorse trail) continuing down to a bridge over the River Amber. Climb up the track, turning left at the road, then immediately right at junction, up the road past the church, continuing until you reach the car park.

Walk 5
Eddlestow 1

This is a harder walk with a few hills. There is attractive scenery, especially the wooded track down to Kelstedge and many areas with open views of the surrounding countryside. A doctor's ghostly experience on a foggy night recalls a strange sad tale from long ago.

Distance: 10 miles.

Grade: B.

Parking: From the A632 Matlock/Chesterfield Road, at Top Slack Farm take road signposted Darley Dale and Beeley. Then take first right, signposted Picnic Area and Uppertown. Car park is a couple of hundred yards down this road on the right.

Map Ref: SK324632. Outdoor Leisure 24 White Peak Area.

Pub Stop: The Red Lion, Stone Edge (on B5057).

Route

1. Turn right out of car park. Where road bends left, turn right down a stony track, continuing down through a pleasant wooded area for about 1¼ miles to the road at Kelstedge. (T-junction at end of Vernon Lane.)

2. Turn left and then immediately right on to The Causeway. Continue to the next road, where you turn right, and then a few yards further on, turn left on to the track. Continue on this track and after about ¼ mile, after passing a track on the left, which joins, at 8 o'clock, the track you are on, turn left at a footpath in the hedge on the left (just before footpath sign on the right). Follow the wall on your right, going through the stile straight ahead and continue up the field with the wall now on your left.

On reaching the next road, turn right, then immediately left up Chapel Hill. A short distance further on, where roads join, ignore the two roads to the right and go straight on up the lane ahead, where 'Moorcroft' is carved on an old millstone on the left.

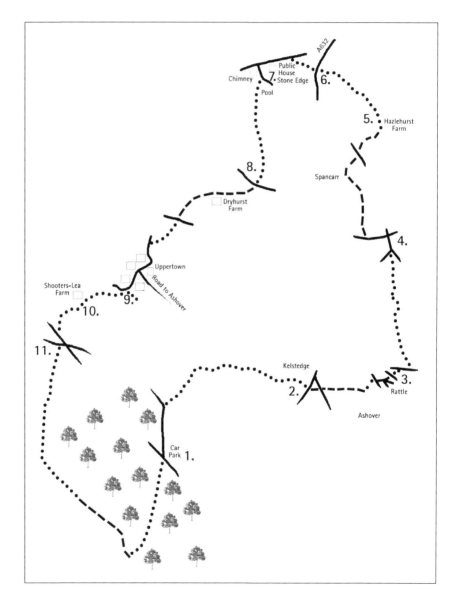

The area that you have just passed through is called Rattle and was where the framework knitters of the lace trade, lived in the 19th century. Its name possibly derives from the noise of the frames being worked.

3. Before a gate, turn left up a track to the left of a wall, to a road, where you turn right and then left at the footpath sign. (This is a nice place for a coffee stop with good views looking back towards Ravensnest Tor and Cocking Tor). You now have ten fields to cross and to help you keep track I have numbered them.

In this first field, follow the wall on your left and about halfway along, cross the wall and continue in the same direction; In the second field the wall is now on your right. At the end, cross into the third field and turn left at 10 o'clock to cross this field. Continue across the fourth field in the same direction, going through a gap in the wall on the far side. In the fifth field turn right, and proceed with the wall on your right. In the sixth field walk straight across and over the stile. In the seventh field turn left along the wall to the end of the field, then turn right and then left through the stile.

In the next (eighth) field, go right diagonally to 2 o'clock to a point midway along the wall. Go through the stile and continue in the same direction, crossing the corner of the ninth field to the stile in the hedge. Continue in the same direction over the tenth and last field to its corner and on to the road.

4. At the road, go straight on, then turn left at the main road. After passing two fields on the right-hand side, turn right on to a track. Stay on the track to farm. Just before the farm entrance, turn left on to the footpath over the stile. Go straight ahead, following a wall on the right, over a stile, then diagonally right, heading to the right of a cottage. Go through a gate and to the stile in a wall on the right-hand side. In the next fields, continue in same direction through stiles to a lane. Go straight over lane (Highashes Lane) on to a track down to Hazelhurst Farm.

5. On reaching farmyard, turn left into the field. Follow wall on the left, then when wall finishes, go diagonally right to the bottom right-hand corner. Continue straight ahead, towards buildings but just before you reach them, go left through a stile. Turn right and ahead to the stile in right corner. Turn left on the track then right over another stile.

Bear right to the stile and on to the narrow path to the next stile. Go to the left of the hedge, then straight ahead, crossing the field to the stile in the wall. (Indistinct as it has half collapsed). Over this stile and into the bracken – the track is rather unclear and can be overgrown by bracken in summer and autumn – but it winds through, eventually turning left to the road.

6. Go straight over at the road on to the track opposite. This is a good picnic lunch spot if you wish to eat before reaching the pub. Continue on the track, following the wall, going past some buildings to reach the Red Lion pub car park.

Coming out of the pub, turn left down the road to a minor road. Turn left here.

7. Go up this road to the footpath sign and turn right past the pool on your left.

The chimney on your right is Stone Edge Chimney built *c.*1770 and is the oldest industrial chimney in Britain. It was restored in 1979. There is a plaque with further details for those interested.

At the end of the pool, bear left on to a muddy track (it may be overgrown depending on season). Passing to the right of next pools, continue to the stile in the wall. Continue in same direction and go ahead on path across moorland. When you reach a wall, continue with wall on the left-hand side to the stile in corner (hidden behind gorse bush at time of writing).

Follow direction indicated by arrow across next field to the stile in corner (situated to the right of gateway). In next field bear right towards gate to the stile in the wall to the left of gate. Bear slightly right and then left down grass track to the road.

8. On reaching road turn right, then left to Dryhurst Farm, staying on the track to the road. Turn left at the road, then right on to the footpath, (by small breezeblock building). Follow fence on the left and where fence ends, bear right at 45° to the stile in fence/wall. Continue with fence on the left for one field, then diagonally right at the sign across the field to the road.

Turn left through Uppertown. Continue through houses and pass a lane on the left, signposted Kelstedge/Ashover.

In 1948, Dr Bell, was called out one night at 1.30am and travelled this lane from Ashover to Uppertown. He encountered a fog unlike any he had ever experienced before. It was so dense that it even came into the car until he could see nothing. Though he was a logical man, he was unnerved by it, as he knew it was unnatural. Thankfully it cleared and he was able to continue on his way.

The Uppertown/Ashover Road where a doctor encountered a ghostly fog.

There is said to be a tale of a man in this area who, long ago, wanting help for his wife, who was about to give birth, went out seeking a doctor. It was a foggy night and unable to find a doctor, he returned to find his wife and baby dead. He was said to be heartbroken and died also within a year. Was Dr Bell's foggy experience a recreation of that other foggy night long ago, triggered perhaps by the association of him being a doctor? Experts say that mist is often a manifestation of a ghost, more so apparently than a ghostly body.

9. Having passed the lane, take **second** footpath to the left. Cross stream using stepping stones and go through stile ahead.

Follow trees on the left to arrow post and turn left through holly trees. Then bearing slightly right, go up the hill to the stile. Cross paved track and go straight across the field to Shooters Lea Farm, through gates, turning left down drive. At end of drive, turn 180° right over the stile and over footbridge.

10. Turn right across the field, then at next stile, turn left up the hill. Continue on this path up the hill until you reach the road. Turn left at the road and right at junction.

11. After a short distance, take footpath to the left and go straight across five fields. In the sixth, continue in the same direction, heading for the right-hand corner of a wood. (Beyond the wood on the horizon Riber Castle may be seen in the distance). Turn left and go along edge of wood. Go over the stile on to grassy track. Continue straight ahead on the lane (Cuckoostone Lane) which leads back into the trees. Where the wood on the left finally ends, turn left at the footpath sign.

The path follows a wall on the right and then bears left on to a broad track through trees. Keep straight on where a track crosses your track and continue ahead to the road. Go straight over on to the road opposite and go down this road to the car park on the right.

Walk 6
Eddlestow 2

A 9-mile walk in an area to the west of Ashover, through a variety of woods, fields and escarpments, which has wonderful views of the Amber Valley. Ghostly interest is provided at the church in Ashover, with a headless woman and a haunted coffin.

Distance: 9 miles.

Grade: B.

Parking: From the A632 Matlock/Chesterfield Road, at Top Slack Farm take road signposted Darley Dale and Beeley. Then take first right signposted Picnic Area and Uppertown. Car park is a couple of hundred yards down this road on the right.

Map Ref: SK324632. Ordnance Survey Pathfinder 761 Chesterfield.

Pub Stop: Crispin Inn, Ashover.

Route

1. Turn left out of the car park, up the road. Go straight over the road into the wood. Keep straight ahead through wood and after crossing second broad track, go left where the paths fork. Continue, going on to a narrower path with a wall on your left and finally reaching a tarmacked track on the edge of the wood. Turn left here and then left again when you reach the road.

2. Turn right at Public Footpath sign to Tansley and Ashover. Follow yellow arrow through two gates, then follow fence and wall on the left across the field and in the next field, heading for the buildings and stile in the top right corner. Go through a wooded area, then across three fields to a road. Cross this road and continue straight ahead, going down a field and up the next one. Go through a stile and turn left to go along the top of the next

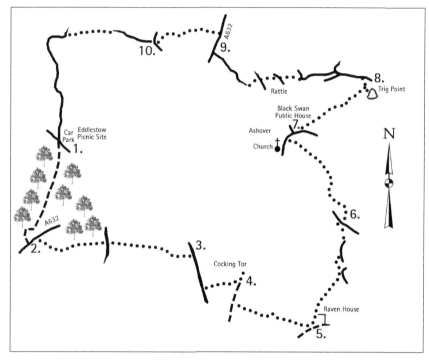

field with a wall on the left, then go left, passing to the left of the water, through a stile, then up the hill, going to the left of Old Engine Farm to the road.

3. Turn right on the road, passing the farm with its millstones. Take second footpath on the left, opposite Holestonemoor Farm, across two fields, then turn right following footpath sign. Continue round to the rocks below Cocking Tor, where there are wonderful views over the Amber Valley. This is a good place for a coffee stop. Ogston Reservoir may be seen in the near distance and on a clear day, on the horizon, Hardwick Hall may be glimpsed. Continue down this path bearing right at fork on to a broader track.

4. Turn right up the track up the hill. Ignore a stile to the left near the bottom. On approaching a wood near the brow of the hill, turn left, through a partially hidden gap in the wall at the top of a steep bank and over the stile. Go down the field, past a large stone trough, then through a stile on edge of

the trees and continue down, winding through trees, in the same direction. Cross the grassy area and go over a stile and down a path to the left of the building, but then turn right across front of the buildings to a waymarked stile. From waymark, continue in direction indicated for three fields. In fourth field, head for stile 20 yards to the left of a gap in the hedge, leading on to a broad grassy track.

5. Turn left and then left again over a stile before buildings (Raven House). Follow the hedge on the right across the field, then across three more fields to the road. Turn left and then left at the footpath sign at side of Miners Arms pub and ahead on to path. Go right where the paths fork, continuing at the side of the stream, bearing round to the right over the stream to the road. Turn left and then left at Public Bridleway, bearing right on to a lane. Turn right at the stile over the bridge over the stream, then on reaching a broad track, turn right up to the road. Turn right.

6. Turn left at the footpath sign and left on path. Follow fence on the left past a quarry then turn left through stile into a wooded area. Continue through the wood, then into a more open area. Then on reaching next stile, follow the wall on your right. Continue ahead, eventually reaching a broader path which leads to the road in Ashover opposite the Crispin Inn, your pub stop.

There is a record of there being a church at Ashover in *Domesday Book.*

A headless woman is said to haunt the churchyard, last officially recorded as being seen in 1890, when spotted in the north aisle of the church at 8pm by a local. The ghost is said to be the wife of a farmer, John Townrow, who in 1841 bludgeoned her to death before cutting off her head and then slitting his own throat.

Some years before this last apparition, in 1879, a skull was found by a workman at Stubben Edge Hall, which is south of Ashover. One theory is that the skull was removed from Ashover churchyard for a wager and taken to the hall and the headless spectre is therefore searching for her head.

An empty stone coffin in the church is also believed to be haunted. If you walk round the empty coffin three times, then lie within it with your eyes closed, it is said you will then hear the ghostly sounds of rattling chains, faintly at first and then more loudly.

7. Turn right, then passing a road on the left and The Black Swan pub, turn left on a footpath up the field, on to a narrow track, going through some tunnels to a lane. Turn left, then right over a wooden stile and continue up the field to the brow of the hill. Turn right along to a trig point and marker pointing out all the points of interest from this fantastic viewpoint.

8. Return back the way you came along the ridge and continue straight ahead until you are near the road on your right, where you join the road. Where the road forks at Hillside, take the right-hand road. Ignore the road leading off to the right and continue ahead. Ignore footpaths to the right and left and then after passing a cottage, turn left at a footpath sign, dropping down and then continuing with a wall on the left. Where the wall ends, bear left down a field to a stile in the wall. Go straight over a road, keeping left where the road forks, down to a lane. Turn right, then left at the footpath sign, then go down a field with the wall on your right, through a stile and, with wall now on the left, continue down to a lane. Turn right and keep straight ahead (ignoring footpath to the left) along a broad track, crossing a stream and continuing ahead until you reach the main road (A632).

9. Turn right. Just before footpath sign, turn left through a gap in the wall, and go straight up between fence and trees. Continue ahead with wall on the left in first field, then straight ahead now with wall on the right in second and into third field. Part of the way down third field, turn right through gateway with a stile at the side and holly bushes behind the wall. Continue

down the field with a wall on the right to a stile in the corner. Go through gateway and diagonally across next field to the stile near corner, continuing to the road.

10. Turn right and follow road marked Uppertown. Turn left at second footpath sign, up a steep bank and over the stile at top. Then cut across corner of field to the right to footpath sign and over the stile. Continue over next two fields, then bear right to the stile in corner behind conifers. Follow hedge on the left to the stile by the gate, then go left over the stile opposite barn. Follow direction of arrow to fingerpost, where you go straight ahead (**not right**). Continue across the fields following arrow signs until you reach the road. Turn right and climb the hill, following sign at junction for Tansley and Wessington. Continue on road back to car park.

Walk 7
Millthorpe

This is a lovely walk through a variety of woodlands and fields with fine views, showing the rural Derbyshire countryside at its best. The woods are full of bluebells and wild garlic in spring, lush with growth in summer and full of colour in autumn.

It is an area full of old fashioned and intriguing place names denoting its occupation over many centuries. A ghostly dog and two haunted halls, Woodthorpe and Fanshawe Gate Hall, add to the interest. The gardens of Fanshawe Gate Hall may be visited in summer. (For details see end of walk.)

Distance: 9¼ miles.

Grade: B.

Parking: Park on Millthorpe Lane in the village of Millthorpe, which lies on the B6051 road from Chesterfield to Owler Bar.

Map Ref: SK318765. Ordnance Survey Pathfinder 761 Chesterfield.

Pub Stop: The George and Dragon or The Angel, Holmesfield, reached after 6 miles.

Route

1. Go down the road opposite Millthorpe Lane, which is Mill Lane. Cross ford by bridge and continue straight ahead, ignoring footpath right. Go left at stile by the gate, then right following hedge on the right, over wooden bridge and stile and back into the field. Continue with the hedge/fence on the right as it bears left up the hill, going over the stile by the gate at top. Continue straight ahead through gate to the right of buildings to lane, known as Johnnygate Lane. Turn right, then left at the footpath sign, going over the stile, bearing slightly left across the field, walking on the right-hand side of hedge, and going over the stile into wood. Go through wood then

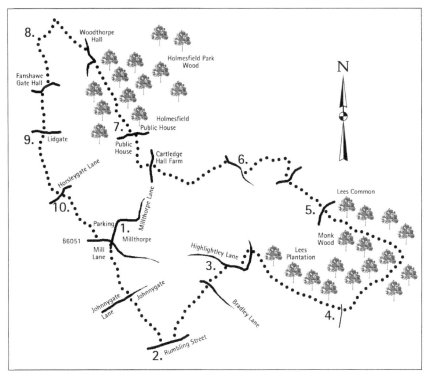

cross fields, to the stile by iron gate and bear right up the track, over the stile past farm to the road.

This has the lovely old fashioned name of Rumbling Street! It was, no doubt, named for the noise of carriages rumbling along.

2. Turn left on road, then left at the footpath sign for Bradley Lane. Follow fence/hedge on the left to stone stile. Go straight ahead with hedge on the right. Continue across the fields to the stile and road (Bradley Lane). Turn left, then right at the footpath sign, down lane, then through right-hand gate stile, following hedge on the right-hand side and up the field to the stile on to lane.

3. Turn right (Highlightley Lane), going through buildings, then just past Brindwoodgate Cottage on the left, turn left at the footpath sign on to

another lane, then right down grassy track by hen houses. Continue past a very attractive property on the right, going up steps into trees and continuing up the hill to the road. Turn right, then left up the lane before post box. Go right at fork through stile by the gate on to woodland track. (Lees Plantation). Continue on this very pleasant path, later passing several pools on the right, (ignoring path to the right at this point) coming into an open area, and eventually reaching a car park on your right.

4. Go straight ahead following footpath sign, following Dunstan Brook on your right, but then bear left over the bridge and crossing a path, go up the hill. Go over the stile into the field, then bear diagonally right to top right-hand corner (i.e. not on path to the right). On reaching the corner, go through the left-hand iron gate, then in next two fields, follow the hedge on the right, to a stile into the wood. Go straight ahead on a winding path in the wood. A little further on, where the path forks, take the left-hand fork. On joining a broad track, turn left and continue on this path for about ½mile, to a stile by a wooden gate. Then continue on the edge of wood, going to the left of houses and down drive and a lane to the road at Lees Common.

5. Go straight over road, following footpath sign, over a stile and follow fence on the left for one field. Go over the stile into next field, then diagonally across the field, into another field continuing in same direction. In next field, follow hedge round to the right to the stile leading on to the road. Turn left on road and then right at stile opposite One Ash Farm. Go along edge of field with hedge on the right and then, on reaching a crossroad of paths, turn left and proceed with a hedge on your left for 1½ fields, then go across the corner of the remainder of the second field. Go ahead to the right of the wood, continuing with trees on the left and then ahead to corner. Go on to wide track and ahead to lane on to the road.

6. Turn right, then left at the footpath to Holmesfield sign. Go down field into dip and across planking and up other side. Across next field and copse and stream, then diagonally left in following field to the stile by the gate. Then go right following hedge on the right and continuing straight ahead in next field to the track. If you look behind at this point there is an excellent view on a clear day, with the twisted spire of Chesterfield Church to be seen in the middle distance.

Although the twist is supposed to be due to unseasoned timbers being used, a better story is that the Devil rested on it whilst travelling to Derby, twining his tail around the spire. A wedding was taking place in the church below and when the bride and groom emerged, the Devil was so surprised to see that the bride was a virgin that he twisted round for another look!

Turn right past Cartledge Hall Farm to the road. Turn left then right following footpath to 'Unthank.'

The unusual name of Unthank does not refer to ingratitude, but denotes land held against the will or without the owner's consent. i.e. a squatter's holding.

Go down the track to the stile by the gate and continue down field, crossing bridge over stream. Then turn right following sign for Holmesfield Church. Go up next field parallel to hedge on the left then over the stile, on to grassy track to the road and a choice of the pubs, The George and Dragon or The Angel, across the road.

Holmesfield is said to have been haunted by a ghostly black dog, with enormous eyes, whose appearance at crossroads foretold death. Dogs of all sizes are reported as apparitions in many different situations. Some are gentle and protective, whilst others are large and fearsome with huge eyes.

7. Facing the Angel pub, go up the lane to the left of it, marked 'Footpath to Woodthorpe Hall and Totley.' Continue on to a footpath, which leads on to a track through a wood for just under ½ mile to the road. Turn right on road, then left at the footpath sign (hidden in trees) by a gateway.

To the right lies Woodthorpe Hall, where one of the downstairs rooms has a 'presence'. A former housekeeper, cleaning in the room heard and felt someone come into the room behind her but when she turned around there was no one there.

At a meeting held in the same room, one of the women was convinced of a presence in the room and, in spite of there being a roaring fire in the grate, sat and shivered all evening. The room in question was one in which members of the family were laid out prior to a funeral.

Go down field, over the stile, then follow wall on the right and bear left (not into lane) over another stile. Bear slightly left across the field, then bear right through wood. Cross bridge over stream and ahead for a short distance, then turn left on a broad path.

After approximately ¼ mile, where you can see an open field on the right through the trees, look for a fairly broad path on the **left-hand** side. The path is a little hard to spot. It is situated at a point, which is ⅔rds of the way along the open field to be seen to the right. This path drops down and bears left to a bridge over a stream, which is your confirmation that this is the correct path.

8. On far side of the bridge, go over the stile and bear right up the field to the right of a line of trees, then going through an open gateway. Continue on the left side of a fence to a stile in that fence. Go over the stile and ahead up the field, still with fence on your right. Go over the stile to the left of barn and pause here for a rest, making use of the seat the owners have placed for ramblers.

This is Fanshawe Gate Hall, which has a history dating back to 1260, being owned by the Fanshawe family from then until 1944. Henry Fanshawe became Remembrancer of the Exchequer to Queen Elizabeth I in 1566 and the architecture of the main hall is predominantly 16th-century. The cottage to the left is part of the original 13th-century hall, with the dovecote beyond it being 14th-century. The present hall will be seen as you continue on your way passing the main hall gates.

The present occupants, John and Cynthia Ramsden, have lived here since 1959 and have spent the intervening years renovating the house and gardens. They tell me that soon after they moved in, at the end of January 1961, they were reading in bed at 11.45pm, when they heard three distinct knocks on their bedroom door. Mr Ramsden got up thinking it was their

Fanshawe Gate Hall, where ghostly hands tap you on the back!

German au pair but found no one there. He checked the house, the au pair was in her room and there was no wind or other reason for the noise. He settled down to sleep, but his wife remained awake and again heard the three knocks on the door but this time the sound was fading away.

On another occasion, their cleaner at the time, Sybil, was using a vacuum cleaner in this corridor and felt someone tap her on the shoulder. She turned expecting it to be Mrs Ramsden telling her coffee was ready, but there was no one there. She arrived downstairs white as a sheet and very much in need of that cup of coffee! A friend of the Ramsdens who stayed with them, said he felt a presence in the corridor when he got up in the night.

Trish Boden, their present housekeeper, told me that she was using a vacuum cleaner in one of the bedrooms and felt something (like two hands) touch her at the bottom of her back. She thought she had backed into some piece of furniture until she turned and realised nothing was there.

However, she says that she did not feel frightened and Mr and Mrs Ramsden report that the house has a happy atmosphere so any spirits within it must be contented.

The Ramsdens open their gardens to the public in summer. For details see end of walk.

Go on to the track bearing left to the road. Turn right on the road and past the attractive entrance of Fanshawe Gate Hall.

The Fanshawe coat of arms is incorporated into the wrought iron gates and the wind vane of the dovecote.

Turn left at the footpath sign and continue up this track with a fence on your right to a road at Lidgate.

9. Cross over the road and on to a footpath on the opposite side. Go ahead with the fence on your right, then go over the stile in fence on the right and continuing in same direction, head for a stile in a fence to be seen ahead. Bear slightly right in next field, to a stile by a gate and then down another field with a fence on the left, then with a wall on your right. On reaching a footpath sign, turn right down a field to a stile by a gate and ahead in the next field. Go over another stile and on to a road, Horsleygate Lane.

10. Turn left and then right at the footpath sign. Go ahead down stony track through a mobile home park, leaving the track where it bends to the right, to go ahead over a stile. Go straight down next field, going through wooden gate and across a stream and straight down (ignoring stile to the right). Go over another stile and follow footpath sign to 'Millthorpe' heading diagonally left across the field. At bottom corner, turn left through gateway and ahead with hedge on the right. At end of field turn right over the stile in the wall, bearing slightly left across next field, to a stile midway along. Go straight across following field, heading to the left of house, continuing to the road. Turn left on road and continue back to Millthorpe Lane, where you turn left to the car parking.

Worth a visit. Mr and Mrs Ramsden open the gardens of Fanshawe Gate Hall from mid June to the end of July, the proceeds going to various

charities. Their gardens are at their most spectacular in mid summer and are well worth a visit, with a chance to relax over a traditional tea and buy some of the plants they raise from seed.

For dates and times of opening, contact Mr and Mrs Ramsden on: Tel. 0114 289 0391 or Web: www.fanshawegate.org.uk

Walk 8
Baslow

This is a super walk on good paths, tracks and lanes. Two fairly steep ascents (one at the beginning and one after Calver) make it a more energetic walk, but well worth the effort, as you are rewarded with excellent views throughout. A horrible murder, a ghostly dog and a haunted pub help to make it memorable.

Distance: 5¾ miles.
Grade: A/B.
Parking: Pay-and-display car park in the centre of Baslow.
Map Ref: SK258721. Outdoor Leisure 24 White Peak Map.
Pub Stop: Derwentwater Arms, Calver.

Route
1. From car park, turn right, going over a humped back bridge, to view the thatched cottages to be seen to the right.

A long time ago, a tramp called at the door of one of these cottages begging for food. Although the woman of the house was cooking bacon at the time, she told the tramp she had no food to spare for lazy people like himself. This incensed the tramp and knocking her down, he grabbed the pan and poured the boiling fat down her throat, scolding her to death. The tramp was caught and, as punishment for causing such an excruciating death, he was hung in chains from a gibbet by the cottage door, to die slowly of exposure and starvation. His screams over the several weeks he took to die were said to be terrible to hear and could be heard as far away Chatsworth. It is said that in recent years, the screams have been heard by someone hiking across Gibbet Moor, which lies east of Chatsworth.

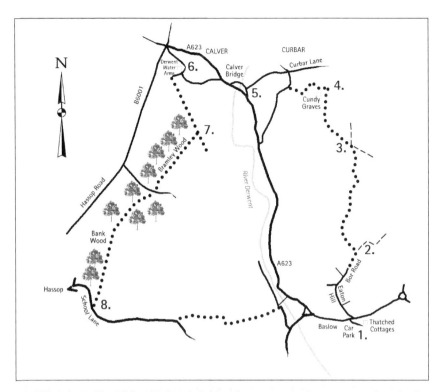

The cottage is said to be haunted by the woman who was murdered. She is described as pleasant-faced and wearing a bonnet. She has appeared at times of illness and leaned over the bedside in concern and the occupant's pain was soothed away.

Return back past the car park and then cross the minor road and then the A619 at the traffic lights. Go up Eaton Hill on the other side. Continue up Eaton Hill until you see the red post box in the wall ahead at a junction. Turn right here up Bar Road. Continue up Bar Road, past the mini island and a road to the left, and as it becomes a stony track. About 100 yards past the end of the houses, you come to a gate on the left, with a stile at the side of it.

2. Go through the stile and ahead on the path. This clear path continues for nearly ¾ mile, first with a wall on your right, then between walls and

Thatched cottages at Baslow, the scene of a horrific murder.

then with a wall on your left. There is a super view of the surrounding countryside. You eventually reach a small ladder stile by an iron gate and a sign for the Eastern Moors Estate.

3. The path divides here. Take the left-hand path. A little further on, the path divides again. Take the left-hand lower path which starts to drop down. Ignore a path going off to the left, stay on the main path. Go through a small iron gate in a wall and continue ahead. Baslow and Curbar Edges may be seen to the right.

When you see some houses ahead, note the little memorial on the left marking the graves of the Cundy family, who died of the plague in 1632. This was, of course, over 30 years before the Great Plague of London, which also devastated Eyam. There is a story concerning the Eagle Stone (see Walk 9) about a William Cundy of Baslow, a man said to be interested in Astronomy, Astrology and a dispenser of herbal remedies. Presumably there is some connection with this family.

4. Just after the little memorial, the path divides. Take the left-hand path and go down and through a gap stile. In the field bear left to a stile by a gate in the bottom right-hand corner. Go ahead across a track and the entrance to Lane Farm. Turn left at the second small gate, and go down between walls. As you reach some houses on the left, pass the first path to the right, then turn right at a second path over a stone stile in the wall. Go ahead with a wall on your left heading for a beech hedge. Continue between houses and go over a stile into a lane where you turn right. Stay on this lane until you reach a junction where you turn left down Curbar Lane. Continue down this lane to the bottom by the church and the Bridge Inn.

5. Turn right on the main road over the little bridge by the sign for Calver.

This area is Calver Bridge, which at one time was quite separate from Calver village. There is a story about a young woman, who was travelling between Calver and Calver Bridge late one night. It was a very dark night and she felt frightened, until she suddenly discovered that she had the company of a white dog, which stayed by her side. Although usually afraid of dogs she found this one friendly and comforting. The dog stayed by her side until the lights of houses were reached, when it went its own way, disconcertingly disappearing through a solid stone wall!

Go ahead past the Craft shop to reach some railings by the road. Cross over the road here and turn right. After 50 yards, just after the telephone box, turn left on a minor road (which is actually Main Street but is unmarked). Continue down this road, which has some very interesting cottages on it, until you reach the commemorative lamp at the end. Turn right and go up Folds Head and round the corner to the Derwentwater Arms.

There is said to be a bedroom in the Derwentwater Arms that regular visitors were loath to sleep in, to the extent that they made some excuse and left if allocated that bedroom. The landlady decided to investigate and to sleep in the double bed in the room with her niece, with a maid in a single bed in the corner. At midnight, the door of the bedroom opened and a

menacing presence entered the room, stopping by the double bed for what seemed an eternity before moving around to the other side and again pausing as though viewing the occupants. When it finally left the room, after a stunned silence, the landlady called to the maid to ask her if she was out of bed. The maid replied no, but she soon would be, and took a flying leap into her landlady's bed, remaining there until morning.

It is said that a previous landlord was a great practical joker, and one night, he got his wife to cover him with a sheet and lay him out as if dead on the table in the parlour. When the customers gathered round to making suitable remarks on his character, he suddenly sat upright frightening them out of their wits. However, by the next night he was laid out again but this time for real as, on the way to Bakewell market he had been thrown from his carriage and broken his neck.

Is the presence in the bedroom anything to do with the prankster landlord?

6. Leaving the pub, turn right to return to the commemorative lamp and then bear right up High Street. Just past the Old Bakehouse, turn left on the public footpath on Folds Lane. On reaching the buildings at the end, turn left towards an iron gate, then right on to a narrow path. Ignore a footpath to the left, then go over a stile into a field. Follow the footpath sign ahead left (not the Calver-Bakewell Road). Go ahead across a large field, continuing where the wall finishes, going down into the dip and continuing in the same direction up the following field. Go over the stile and continue upwards on a path. Bear left as directed at the first arrow sign near to the top.

7. At the next arrow sign turn right, continuing upwards on the last bit of climbing. There is a wonderful view at this point, looking back over Calver and to the Edges. Continue on this path, with a fence/wall on your left, for ½ mile until you reach a wooden gate leading on to a lane (Bramley Lane). Turn left and immediately right over a stile on the far side and on to a broad path through woodland. Turn right at the yellow marker, going over the wall and turning left, following the sign for School Lane and Hassop. Go ahead again with a wall on your left. When this path, after ¾ mile, eventually

reaches an open field, go over the stile and follow the direction of the arrow sign across the field to a lane.

8. Turn left and stay on this lane for ½ mile, until, where the road swings to the right, you turn left at a Public Footpath sign. Follow its direction across the field, to a yellow arrow directing you to the stile in the bottom left-hand corner. Go straight down the next field following a wall on your left. Over a stile into a third field. On reaching a wall at the end of this field, turn right along it (briefly joining another path). At the end of the wall turn left, again keeping the wall on your left-hand side. Continue down the field and over the stile into the next. Keep straight ahead over the next three fields, then over a stile and down a narrow path to a road. Turn right and on reaching a road at the end, turn left. Cross over and turn right at the junction. Stay on this road until, just past the Cavendish Hotel, you turn right on to the minor road to the car park.

Walk 9
Curbar Gap

An easy 10-mile walk, on clearly defined paths. The outward route is along Baslow and White Edges and it returns along Froggatt and Curbar Edges, giving excellent views throughout. Curbar Gap, its starting point, was an important crossroads for some of the ancient packhorse routes across Derbyshire, and an 18th-century guidepost may be seen, together with a 'clapper' bridge later in the walk. The haunted Eagle Stone, with its strange tales is also visited.

Distance: 10 miles.

Grade: A.

Parking: At Curbar Gap pay-and-display car park. From roundabout just outside Baslow, take A621 Baslow to Sheffield road. After one mile, turn left on minor road signposted Curbar. The car park is on the right after approximately one mile.

Map Ref: SK263747. Outdoor Leisure 24 White Peak Area.

Pub Stop: The Grouse Inn. Also refreshments are available at Longshaw Lodge.

Before starting the walk, take a minute to examine the guidepost situated in the field to the left of the car park. This guidepost is evidence of the packhorse ways that converged on Curbar Gap. An Act of Parliament in 1702 ordered guideposts to be set up where routes crossed, with the name of the next market town being in the direction the side faces. This guidestone has on its sides: Shefield (sic) Rd; Dronfield Rd; Chesterfield Rd; Tidswall (sic) Rd and a date 1709. One can imagine how comforting it must have been to come across a guidepost like this, to confirm's one's route in poor visibility, in times when only packhorse trails spanned Derbyshire.

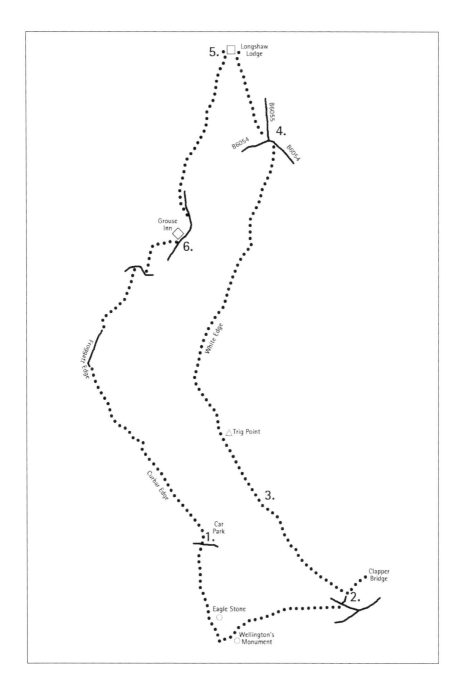

Route

1. Returning to the road, turn right then bear left up a track. Go through a gate into Eastern Moors Estate and straight ahead on a broad track. This is Baslow Edge. After about ½ mile a large rock, the Eagle Stone is reached on the left.

The Eagle Stone may be named after Aigle, a giant Celtic god, whose favourite activity seemed to be tossing huge boulders around the countryside. Alternatively, it may come from the word Egglestone, meaning Witch Stone. According to legend, on certain days of the year, at cock crow, this haunted stone is said to turn around.

The Eagle Stone is said to turn around at dawn.

Also, there used to be a tradition that the girls of the village of Baslow would not accept the courtship of any young man until he had proved himself by climbing the Eagle Stone. Young men who succeeded in scaling the stone to the top were thought to be looked upon favourably by the spirit which dwelt within the stone.

Another strange story attached to the Eagle Stone concerns a William Cundy of Baslow, a man said to be interested in Astronomy, Astrology and a dispenser of herbal remedies. One day a child had gone missing and the countryside had been searched to no avail. As a last resort the parents asked William for help. He made mysterious calculations and announced that the child would be found asleep beneath the shadow of the Eagle Stone, with her bonnet by her side. The father rushed to the Stone and found his daughter asleep and of course, by her side, was her bonnet!

Just beyond this stone, turn left on a path to pass Wellington's Monument. Continue ahead on this broad path, for about a mile, passing a wood and some dry stone walling, until you reach the road.

2. Crossing the road, go over a stile and take the track bearing right. After about 100 yards, you will come to a stone 'clapper' bridge over Bar Brook.

There are two long slabs of stone with a date 1742 on top of one of them. The name clapper bridge is said to derive from the Latin for a 'heap of stones'.

The paving of the original packhorse route can be seen leading down and up the other side. Further to the left is a wider paved track 5-6ft wide leading out of the brook, presumably a later ford used by wagons. This crossing of Bar Brook was referred to as Saltersford as far back as 1614. A salter was a carrier of salt by packhorse.

After visiting the bridge, return back up the track to a short guidepost where you turn right. Keep ahead on this broad path following the guideposts. Further on, the path curves round the side of a hill and then bears left over a wooden plank bridge and continues ahead to a footpath sign. (From the clapper bridge to the sign approximately one mile.)

3. At footpath sign, follow sign for Longshaw. Keep straight ahead on this well-defined path, passing a trig point on the hill to the right after about ½ mile. The path continues for another 1½ miles. On reaching a wall with a footpath continue to follow the sign for Longshaw. (Do not be tempted by the sign for the Grouse Inn, which comes later in the

walk!). Where a path crosses your own, keep straight ahead and continue until you reach the road.

4. Turn left on the Sheffield Road, then almost immediately turn left through a gate stile at the National Trust sign for Wooden Pole. Go straight ahead on a broad grassy track. On reaching a white metal gate on the left, go through gate stile at the side of it, on to a stony track through the trees. On reaching the buildings, follow the track round to the left to the front of Longshaw Lodge. This is a good place for a lunch stop. Refreshments, WCs and a National Trust shop are all well worth a visit.

5. On leaving the Lodge, go ahead, then left on the footpath. Go through a small gate and bear left through a second gate (ignoring path to the right). Go ahead on to a broad path. Ignore a path that crosses your own and continue ahead until you reach the road, where you turn right. Stay on the road (ignoring stile on the right) until you reach the Grouse Inn.

6. Coming out of the Grouse Inn, turn right and almost immediately right again over a stile. Go diagonally left across three fields, cross a stile then turn left on a path passing a car park on your left. Go down into a dip, across a stream and up to a road. On reaching the road, turn right, then bear left through gate stile on to a track. This broad well-defined path continues for about 2½ miles along Froggatt Edge and Curbar Edge to bring you eventually back to the car park.

Walk 10
Great Longstone 1

A fairly easy walk, over a variety of scenery, using footpaths, fields and tracks and some moorland. It takes in the attractive steep-sided Coombs Dale, which is most attractive in May time with lovely wildflowers, cowslips, purple orchids, bluebells and gorse. It also passes a chasm, which is 300 million years old.

A highwayman, a haunted mine, the ghost of a jilted maiden and a protective ghostly dog add to its enjoyment.

Distance: 10 miles.
Grade: A/B.
Parking: Main Street, Great Longstone, near War Memorial.
Map Ref: SK420718. Outdoor Leisure 24 White Peak Area.
Pub Stop: Moon Inn, Stoney Middleton.

Route.

1. Go up Station Road between the War Memorial and the Crispin pub. Turn right at the footpath sign and follow path across five fields. In fifth field bear right slightly, heading for buildings to be seen ahead. On reaching road, turn left, then turn right at the footpath sign at The Packhorse Inn, at Little Longstone.

2. Go over the stile to the left of gate. In the first field, keeping to the wall on the right-hand side, cross this wall by the stile halfway along. In second field keep wall on your left. In third field head at 1 o'clock to the stile. In fourth field go straight ahead to the stile in the wall. Go over the stile and continue, keeping wall on the left-hand side. Where wall on the left finishes, follow wall on the right-hand side for two fields. Crossing into next field, bear left to 11 o'clock to the stile leading on to the track.

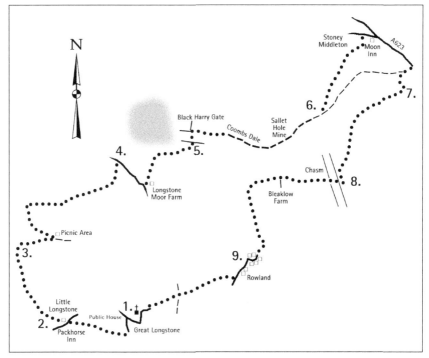

3. Turn right on the track. After ½ mile, at picnic area on the left, turn sharp left up the track. On reaching wall, turn right crossing it by the stile in the corner. Turn right up the field following wall. A few yards after reaching the end of this wall, turn right through gap on to grassy track leading up the hill. Keep to the right of the first trees, then to the left of second group, staying on a grassy track going straight ahead.

A broad track crosses your track and, just beyond, where the track forks, take the left-hand fork, again on a grassy track. On reaching a stony track turn left to the road.

4. On the road, turn right. Turn left at the footpath sign to Longstone Moor Farm. Passing to the left of the farm, continue straight ahead, keeping fence on the right-hand side. On reaching footpath sign, cross the wall to the right and go straight ahead, keeping fence on the right-hand side. On reaching the end of the fence, bear left at 11o'clock to footpath sign in the wall. Turn left keeping the wall on the right.

5. Go through the gate, cross first track, then turn right on to second into Coombs Dale.

This is known as Black Harry Gate, named after a highwayman called Black Harry, who, in the early 18th century frequently attacked and robbed the packhorse trains that crossed the moors in that area.

Continue down Coombs Dale, an attractive steep sided dale, dotted with old mine workings.

Coombs Dale was previously mined for lead. It is now worked for fluorospar and barytes, used in chemical, paint and paper manufacturing, textiles, rubber and oil industries.

After about ¾ mile, you will be passing the Sallet Hole Mine on the left. It is said to be haunted by the ghost of an old man, wearing a cap and a long coat, who is accompanied by a ghostly dog. Both are said to disappear when approached.

6. After about a mile, take footpath to the left. The path goes parallel to the dale and then climbs up by a rocky crag. At the top there is a good view of the dale below. Turn right and then left on path, then bear right through trees, again parallel to the dale, to a

The cliff at Stoney Middleton, haunted by a jilted maiden.

stile in a wall. Go across four fields, then follow direction of footpath sign to Stoney Middleton. Go to bottom of field, through the garden and continue down to the track. On reaching the track turn left and continue to the road. Turn right and the pub, the Moon Inn, is at the bottom of the hill.

Stoney Middleton is popular with rock climbers due to its limestone cliff faces. It has a Lover's Leap Rock, where Hannah Badaley, jilted by her lover, leapt in 1762, down an 80-foot cliff face. The winds made her skirts billow out like a parachute and she landed 'safely' in some thorn bushes. However, she is said to have died of a broken heart some two years later, aged 26. Her ghost is said to be seen, still wandering on the hillside, in a re-enactment of her original attempt to take her life.

Coming out of the pub turn right on to the A623.

On this road from Calver Sough to Stoney Middleton, a Methodist minister was walking one night, having collected money from the various chapels, which he served. Unknown to him, he was being followed by two robbers, bent on relieving him of his collection money, when he was joined by a large dog, which, protectively followed at his heels until he reached Stoney Middleton. Concerned that the dog might get lost, he tried to use his walking stick to gently direct the dog back to its home, at which point he was disconcerted to find that his stick passed straight through it!

Continue along the A623 to playing fields on the right. Turn right on a track on the left side of a field marked 'Private Road'. Turn left on to the footpath – up steps. Go left through wooden gate and straight ahead to a track by two iron gates.

7. Turn right up the track and continue climbing steadily up, over the stile and going straight ahead on a broad grassy track curving left, and coming eventually to another stile. Cross stile and continue up the track. On reaching way marker on the right, continue straight ahead on stony track, winding left and right, crossing chasm (best seen to the right) which is 300 million years old!

8. Go to the right to the track by trees. Continue past entrance to Bleaklow Farm and just after the end of the trees, on seeing two tracks together on the left-hand side, turn left on to the right-hand track, passing down between walls. Continue to the end, then turn right on stony lane to the houses at Rowland.

9. On nearing the end of the village, passing Rake's Barn on the left, take footpath to the right. Cross five fields, then go straight over a green lane (Handrake Lane). Cross three more fields leading on to another green lane. On reaching a stony lane, turn left and then turn right at the road, going past the Church to the main road. Turn right back to parking.

Walk 11
Great Longstone 2

A fairly strenuous 8-mile walk through pleasantly varied countryside between Great Longstone, Eyam and Stoney Middleton, crossing over Coombs Dale, with lovely views of the Dale later in the walk. The walk has some wonderful open scenery.

However, beware, as you may be mown down by a phantom cyclist in Eyam Dale, and your pub stop, The Miner's Arms is said to be the most haunted building in Eyam.

Distance: 8 miles.
Grade: B/C.
Parking: Park on Main Street of Great Longstone, by the war memorial.
Map Ref: SK420718. Outdoor Leisure 24 White Peak Area.
Pub Stop: The Miner's Arms, Eyam or The Moon Inn, Stoney Middleton.

Route

1. Go up narrow road opposite the Post Office and then right on the footpath to Church. Go through the churchyard to the road, where you go straight on and then left at the lane, opposite Croft Lodge. Go straight up the lane and take the second footpath on the right. Follow direction of footpath sign across two fields. Drop down bearing right to a broad track you can see ahead. When you reach a gateway, go to the right of it and up the track. Then turn left over the stile by the gate. Go across this field and up to a stile. There are good views looking back over Great Longstone, towards Ashford-in-the-Water.

2. Continue up the path, which bears right to a track. Go straight over this track (to the left of the stile, not over it) and continue steeply up the hill with fence on your right. Bear slightly left across the field, to a stile in the

middle of fence at the end i.e. not to the stile in top right-hand corner. Go over the stile and across next field to a track. Cross over track and through small iron gate and up the field with wall on your right. Go through gate and continue down bridleway. Through next gate and straight on following the wall on your right. Go past footpath sign to end of field and through next gate, and then go through wooden gate to the right, marked with sign

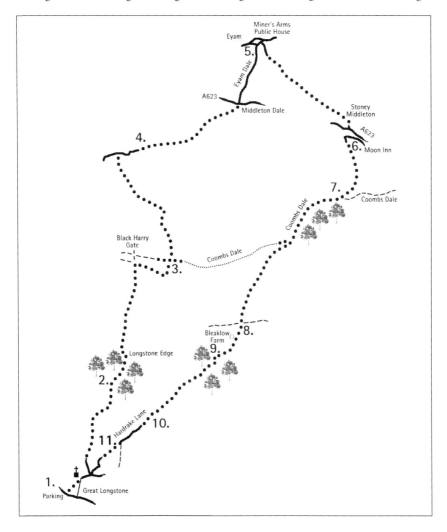

to Hassop Common and Calver. Cross a track and go straight ahead on to a stony track ahead. There is a large field on your right. When you see the wall dividing this field from the next, look for a stile on the **left,** which is just a gap in the wall (only one tall stone remaining). Turn left here and go straight down to Coombs Dale. This is a good place for a coffee stop with good views of the dale below.

3. Having reached the Dale below, cross straight over. The path climbs steeply, bearing to the right, and giving a wonderful view of the Dale below. It then eventually runs alongside a wall on your right. Continue ahead over two stiles until you reach a lane, where you turn right. Turn left at the footpath sign and continue ahead, walking on the left of an embankment. Go over a stile and keep straight ahead ignoring a track to the right. Then at junction, turn right and go down a broad lane until you reach some buildings and a 'Stop' sign. Then turn right following signs for 'Public Highway'. Go up the hill then turn left at the public footpath sign to Eyam Dale.

4. The path bears to the right around the edge of a quarry. Follow the wall as it eventually bears to the right to a stile in the wall. Go over the stile on to a track where you turn left. Continue down the track, until you reach a narrow path straight ahead, which leads down to the main road. Cross straight over and go up Eyam Dale.

Eyam Dale and Stoney Middleton Dale appear to be the haunt of a phantom cyclist. According to reports, two brothers were walking up Eyam Dale when they had to leap out of the way of a cyclist, hurtling down the steep gradient. When

Eyam Dale, haunted by a phantom cyclist.

they turned to make a (no doubt unprintable) comment on his riding, there was no sign of anyone at all!

At this same spot late one night, another witness was startled by the sound of tyres and the agitated ringing of a bicycle bell and hastily moved out of the way, only to be even more startled when nothing appeared.

On another occasion, one of the aforementioned brothers, was walking with his wife, late one night, along Stoney Middleton Dale, when they heard the sound of a decrepit old bike behind them. As they stepped aside to let it pass, an approaching bus lit the road revealing its emptiness!

At yet another time, a cyclist was labouring up Eyam Dale in the pouring rain, when he was amazed to be passed effortlessly by another cyclist. Even more surprising, was the fact that the cape of the other cyclist was perfectly dry, in spite of the downpour!

5. As you reach the village of Eyam, follow the road round to the right to the centre of the village. Ahead left is the Miner's Arms pub. Just before this, on the right, by the side of the telephone box and post box, there is a narrow lane called Lydgate, which is the way your route continues. You may make The Miner's Arms your pub stop or wait until you reach Stoney Middleton which is another ¾ mile.

The Miner's Arms is proclaimed to be the most haunted building in Eyam. Footsteps or running feet are heard upstairs and there have been strange occurrences in the bedrooms, causing some guests to leave hurriedly. One couple is said to have woken in the night, to find the room filled with medical equipment from a bygone age. It is said (somewhat unbelievably) that they went back to sleep and woke in the morning to find it gone and were then so frightened that they left! I think I might have panicked a little earlier if that had been me!

The wife of a former landlord, who was murdered in the 17th century by being thrown down the stairs, is also said to appear, dressed in an old-fashioned bonnet and cape. She is said to have been seen entering the building after it was renovated and wandered about as though confused before disappearing.

The Miner's Arms, claimed to be the most haunted building in Eyam.

Go up the lane between the cottages and note the Lydgate Graves on your right. Where the road goes to the left, follow the footpath sign to Stoney Middleton. Go ahead on a track on the left side of a wall, across a field then on the track between walls. The path then continues across an open field, passing to the right of a clump of trees on a mound and then along a narrow ridge, before dropping down to a lane. Turn right and go down between houses. On reaching another road, turn left and continue ahead.

To the left is the church and behind that is Stoney Middleton Hall. Although no ghosts are reported here, one of the bedrooms is said to be subject to mysterious smells! Persons sleeping there have been awakened by an overpowering smell of sulphur and on one occasion, in the middle of the night, the aroma of bacon and eggs being cooked.

Proceed to a road junction, where you turn right to the Moon Inn, in Stoney Middleton.

6. On leaving the pub, turn left up the hill (High Street) and then left at Eaton Fold. Go along the track and then past Janesway bungalow and through wooden gate. Then through second stile to the left of iron gate. Just before barns, go left over the stile and then right to the stile in fence. Follow the direction of the arrow across the field, on a path which bears to the right, eventually dropping down towards Coombs Dale, where you turn left over a stile into the dale.

7. Turn right in Coombs Dale and continue for ½ mile until you reach a footpath sign on the left. Do not take this path, but a few yards further on, where you pass four iron posts, take an indistinct, unmarked path to the left. Go over a rickety stile and follow the path as it turns to the right and climbs steadily, parallel to the Dale below. The path eventually bears away from the dale and reaches a stile. Go over the stile and ahead, going to the left of a barn. Go over two stiles and ahead to a track.

8. Cross the track and go up the lane to Bleaklow Farm. Go past the farm, going over the stile at the side of a wooden gate. Bear right down field to the stile. Go over the stile, and bear right in second field to another stile by a wooden gate. Go straight ahead through gorse to a track. Cross track bearing right to pick up a wide grassy track, leading on to a stony path.

9. Turn left down this path, then right at stile, following wall on the left. Continue to follow wall where it turns left down the hill to a stile on your left. Bear right across large open field, heading for the corner of two walls jutting into the field from right and past these to the stile to the left of gate in the wall ahead.

10. Go on to grassy track, first heading on an open path then on a path between two walls, but watch for a stile in the wall on the right-hand side after about ¼ mile.

11. Go over the stile and bear left up the field to the stile. Follow footpath sign direction over next field. Then in the following field, bear left to wall on the left and follow it to the corner to the stile leading on to a grassy track. Follow this track, bearing right where a track joins from the left. Cut across corner of field to the left. Go left on the lane and right at the road. Go along past the church to main road, where you turn right back to parking.

Walk 12
Eyam 1

No book of ghost walks could miss Eyam, which must be one of the most haunted villages in England! This is an interesting and pleasant walk, with one steep hill at the start and good views over Eyam. The walk may be 2 or 3 miles depending on whether a diversion to the Riley Graves is made.

Distance: 2 or 3 miles.

Grade: A.

Parking: In the village follow signs for coach and car parking, to reach a pay-and-display car park. WCs available in car park.

Map Ref: SK215768. Outdoor Leisure White Peak Area.

Pub Stop: The Miner's Arms, Eyam.

Route

1. Leave the car park by the entrance and turn right up the hill. Where the main road turns to the right, turn left on to the minor road. Continue ahead where the road becomes a rough track, which zigzags climbing steadily upwards. The path climbs for ½ mile but near the top there are good views over Eyam to distract you. At the top of the path, bear right up to the road where you turn right.

2. Stay on this road, passing a foot - path to the left and one to the right. On reaching a T-junction, turn left following the sign for Mompesson's Well, which is about 50 yards up this road.

Mompesson's Well, Eyam. Haunted by a small boy.

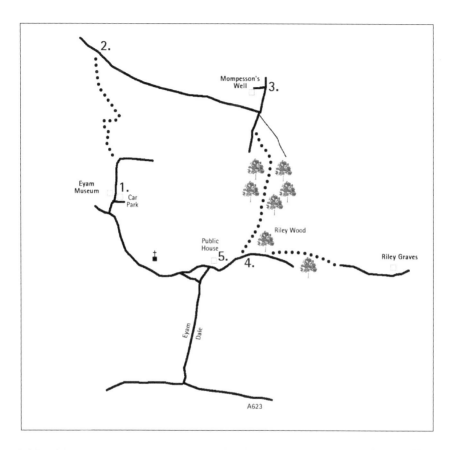

Mompesson's Well is where food and medicine where left for the villagers during the plague. Vinegar was added to the water to disinfect the coins that were left there in payment. The ghost of a small boy is said to be seen nearby.

3. On leaving the well, turn right returning to the junction. Go straight on past the road you have just come down. Then turn left at the public footpath sign into Riley Wood. Where the path divides, take the right-hand path going down. This pleasant woodland path meanders down for ½ mile, eventually reaching a lane, which bears round to the right and then left to the main road.

The Riley graves, Eyam, tended by a ghostly lady in blue.

If you wish to visit the Riley Graves, it will make this a 3-mile walk and involves a gentle climb up to them.

If you do not wish to visit the Riley Graves, turn right on the main road, which will take you back into the centre of Eyam, then follow the instructions at No 5.

4. **To visit the graves.** Turn left on the main road. On reaching a minor road, bear left on to it following a sign for the Riley Graves. When you come to a gateway with stone pillars, again follow sign for the Riley Graves going ahead on a path to the right of the gateway. The Riley Graves are along this track on the left inside the walled enclosure.

The Hancock family of Riley were farmers. During the plague in August 1666, Mrs Hancock tragically buried seven members of her family in eight days. The pain and heartbreak of having to do that, is almost unimaginable and even now, many centuries later, this little cemetery is a sad place to visit. The records show that after the plague she moved to Sheffield.

A blue lady has been seen in the vicinity of the graves and moving amongst them as if tending them, but when people reach the enclosure there is no one there.

Returning to the track, turn right and retrace your route, keeping straight ahead until you reach the main road. Continue along the main road where you will reach the central square of Eyam.

5. The Miner's Arms pub is on the right.

The Miner's Arms is proclaimed to be the most haunted building in Eyam. Footsteps or running feet are heard upstairs and there have been strange occurrences in the bedrooms, causing some guests to leave hurriedly. One couple is said to have woken in the night, to find the room filled with medical equipment from a bygone age. It is said (somewhat unbelievably) that they went back to sleep and woke in the morning to find it gone and were then so frightened that they left! I think I might have panicked a little earlier if that had been me!

The wife of a former landlord, who was murdered in the 17th century by being thrown down the stairs, is also said to appear, dressed in an old-fashioned bonnet and cape. She is said to have been seen entering the building after it was renovated and wandered about as though confused before disappearing.

As you proceed along the main street you will come to the church, which is worth a visit.

In the churchyard, there is a Celtic Cross, which is 8th-century and on the wall an interesting sundial dated 1775.

The tomb of Catherine Mompesson, the wife of Revd Mompesson, is just beyond the Celtic Cross. The Revd Mompesson rallied the villagers to contain the plague and stop it spreading to other villages by isolating themselves in Eyam. He sent his children away but tragically lost his wife. She died on 25 August 1666. Her ghost is said to haunt the rectory and to wander between there and the church, pausing near the Cross. Persons staying at the rectory have heard footsteps in the night as though someone were ill and needing attention.

Eyam church. The ghost of Catherine Mompesson haunts the churchyard and rectory.

Coming out of the churchyard, turn right and as you continue up the main street, you will pass the Plague Cottages and Eyam Hall.

The Plague Cottages, were where the plague was first brought to Eyam in a bundle of cloth and where the first victim died in 1665. The front bedroom of one of the cottages is haunted and a former resident had his sleep disturbed by the ghost so often that he finally refused to sleep there. Described as a pleasant faced lady in a blue smock, he would wake to find her watching him before simply fading away.

In Eyam Hall, which was rebuilt in 1676, one of the upstairs rooms was so incessantly visited by the ghost of an old man that the occupants are said to have kept the door locked. A somewhat futile gesture, if it was to keep the ghost inside, I would have thought, as ghosts seem to have the capacity to travel through walls and doors! However, perhaps it was to keep other people out!

After Eyam Hall, the road bends right and left and you will then reach a sign for the car park, where you turn right and up the hill to the parking.

Walk 13
Eyam 2

This second walk from Eyam is interesting and attractive. You pass the haunted Eyam Hall and the Plague Cottages and through a haunted dell, on the way to Stoney Middleton. The walk then travels through Coombs Dale, which is lovely in springtime for its wildflowers, before returning via the haunted Eyam Dale.

Distance: 6 miles.
Grade: A/B.
Parking: In the village follow signs for coach and car parking, to reach a pay-and-display car park.
Map Ref: SK215768. Outdoor Leisure White Peak Area.
Pub Stop: The Moon Inn, Stoney Middleton.

Route

1. Coming out of the car park entrance, turn left down to the main road and turn left again. Continue down the main street, passing various memorials, Eyam Hall and further on The Plague Cottages, which are on the left, just before the Church.

In Eyam Hall, which was built in 1676, one of the upstairs rooms was so incessantly visited by the ghost of an old man that the occupants are said to have kept the door locked. A somewhat futile gesture, I would have thought, as ghosts seem to have the capacity to travel through walls and doors!

The Plague Cottages, were where the plague was first brought to Eyam in a bundle of cloth and where the first victim died. The front bedroom of one of the cottages is haunted and a former resident had his sleep

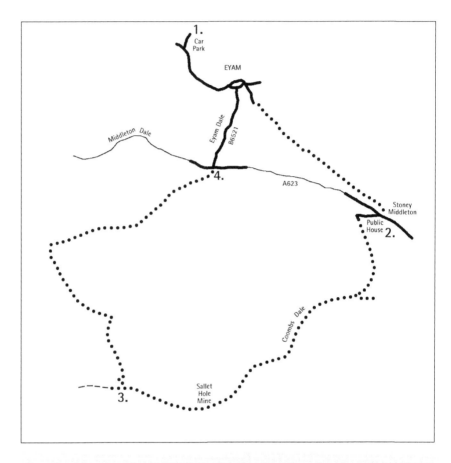

disturbed by the ghost so often that he finally refused to sleep there. Described as a pleasant faced lady in a blue smock, he would wake to find her watching him before simply fading away.

Pass a road junction to the right and then, on reaching the central square, cross over to the right, to a lane adjacent to the telephone box and post box. This is called Lydgate. Go up the lane between the cottages and note the Lydgate Graves on your right. Where the road goes to the left, follow the footpath sign to Stoney Middleton. Go ahead on a track on the left side of a wall, across a field then on a track between walls.

Eyam Hall, with its haunted bedroom.

As you pass down this path, note the derelict cottage to the left, which was haunted by a woman, who would drag the bedclothes off the terrified occupants in the night. Was she connected in some way to the plague and perhaps trying to urge the occupants to get up and leave before it was too late?

She is also said to rush through the dell between here and Stoney Middleton (down which you will be travelling!). Again there seems to be some urgent need that obsesses her. Perhaps the need to escape? One man, returning from the pub, was so frightened by her chasing him that he is said to have given up the demon drink!

The path then continues across an open field, passing to the right of a clump of trees on a mound and then along a narrow ridge, before dropping down to lane. Turn right and go down between houses. On reaching another road, turn left and at junction turn right to the Moon Inn.

2. On leaving the pub, turn left up the hill (High Street) and then left at

Eaton Fold. Go along track and then past Janesway bungalow and through wooden gate. Then go through second stile to the left of iron gate. Just before barns, go left over the stile and then right to the stile in fence. Follow direction of arrow across the field on a path which bears to the right, eventually dropping down towards Coombs Dale, where you turn left over a stile into the dale. Continue up the Dale for 1½ miles.

After about three-quarters of a mile, you will be passing the Sallet Hole Mine on the right. It is said to be haunted by the ghost of an old man, wearing a cap and a long coat, who is accompanied by a ghostly dog. Both are said to disappear when approached.

3. On reaching a footpath sign, turn right. The path climbs steeply, bearing to the right, and giving a wonderful view of the Dale below. It then eventually runs alongside a wall on your right. Continue ahead over two stiles until you reach a lane, where you turn right. Turn left at the footpath sign and continue ahead, walking on the left of an embankment. Go over a stile and keep straight ahead ignoring a track to the right. Then at junction, turn right and go

The Plague cottages, where the plague first came to Eyam.

down a broad lane until you reach some buildings and a Stop sign. Then turn right following signs for Public Highway. Go up the hill then turn left at the public footpath sign to Eyam Dale.

The path bears to the right around the edge of a quarry. Follow the wall as it eventually bears to the right to a stile in the wall. Go over the stile on to a track where you turn left. Continue down the track until you reach a narrow path straight ahead, which leads down to the main road.

4. Cross straight over and go up Eyam Dale.

Eyam Dale and Stoney Middleton Dale appear to be the haunt of a phantom cyclist. According to reports, two brothers were walking up Eyam Dale when they had to leap out of the way of a cyclist, hurtling down the steep gradient. When they turned to make a (no doubt unprintable) comment on his riding, there was no sign of anyone at all!

At this same spot late one night, another witness was startled by the sound of tyres and the agitated ringing of a bicycle bell and hastily moved out of the way, only to be even more startled when nothing appeared.

On another occasion, one of the aforementioned brothers, was walking with his wife, late one night, along Stoney Middleton Dale, when they heard the sound of a decrepit old bike behind them. As they stepped aside to let it pass, an approaching bus lit the road revealing its emptiness!

At yet another time, a cyclist was labouring up Eyam Dale in the pouring rain, when he was amazed to be passed effortlessly by another cyclist. Even more surprising, was the fact that the cape of the other cyclist was perfectly dry, in spite of the downpour!

At the top of Eyam Dale, as you reach the village, bear left on a road signposted 'Coach and car park, Toilets ½ mile.' At the next road, turn left and continue up the main street, back to the road on your right, which leads you back to the car park.

Eyam Museum opposite the car park is well worth a visit for its history of Eyam and the surrounding area and particularly its chilling facts regarding the plague and its symptoms!

Walk 14
Litton

This is a fairly energetic, undulating walk, in the attractive limestone scenery of Cressbrook Dale. Criss-crossing Cressbrook Dale (which means down, up and down!), it rewards with fine views of dramatic countryside and chills with a tale of ghostly hands, should you attempt to rest from your labours!

Distance: 3¾ miles.
Grade: A/B.
Parking: On the main street of Litton village.
Map Ref: SK165752.
Pub Stop: Three Stags' Heads, Wardlow Mires, reached after 2¾ miles.

Route

1. As you come into Litton on the road from the A623, there is a road on the left with a sign pointing to Cressbrook and Monsal Dale, which is the start of your walk. Go down this road. On reaching a right-hand bend, turn left on to a lane and immediately right at a footpath sign. Go over the stile and follow the direction of the sign down the field. Bear left across the corner of the next field, then slightly more to the right in the following field. Go through a gap stile, across a track and over the stile on the far side. Continue across the next field heading for an open gateway. Cross a small field then in the following one, head to the top left-hand corner going through the gap. Continuing in the same direction, head diagonally across the following field to the top corner and a footpath marker. Follow the direction of the yellow arrow over this last field to a stile.

2. Go through the stile and turn right on a path on the edge of woodland. The path follows the wall on your right for ¼ mile. When you reach some man-made steps dropping down left, go down them into the wood. On a reaching a path at the bottom, turn left.

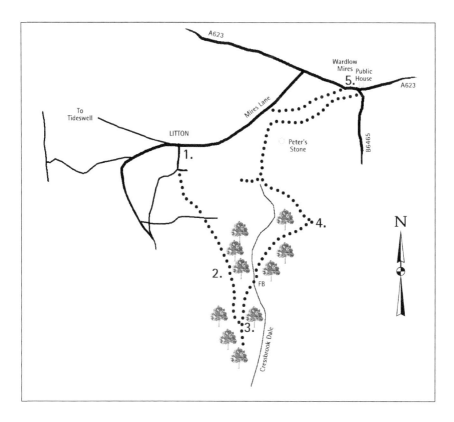

3. Continue along this well marked path. On reaching a stone gateway bear right continuing along the path as it drops down to the dale bottom.

On reaching the path at the bottom, (Cressbrook Dale) go left over the wooden footbridge. Go ahead on this path, then where the paths divide, take right-hand higher path. The path climbs steadily above Cressbrook Dale. At the top, when you see a wall ahead and a path going down to the left, bear left on to this path. There is a lovely view of the dale at this point.

4. Descend to the dale bottom and ignore the footpath to the left, which you reach further along. Continue straight ahead with the wall on your left. As the path climbs above the wall, the rocky limestone outcrop above you to the right is Peter's Stone.

The limestone outcrop of Peter's Stone, where a man was gibbeted for murder.

New Year's Day 1815 was the date on which a toll bar keeper, Hannah Oliver was brutally murdered by Anthony Lingard from Tideswell. Lingard was caught and executed and his body hung in chains from a gibbet on Peter's Stone. Cyclists, in Wardlow Mires (where you are now headed), have reported the touch of invisible hands and the feeling of being strangled as they have rested on the grass verge.

Continue on this broad path for another ½ mile, until you reach a wooden gate leading you on to the road at Wardlow Mires.

If you decide to rest on the grass verge here, watch out for ghostly hands!

5. If you wish to visit the pub, The Three Stags' Heads is a few yards to the right. Otherwise, turn left on the road (turn right coming out of the pub!). After about 100 yards, turn left through a gap stile at a footpath sign. Follow the direction of the arrow to walk with a wall on your right-hand

side. Go over the stile in the wall and head across the next field to the corner, which is to the right of Peter's Stone to be seen in the dale below. Go over the stile and turn right, again with a wall on your right. Go over a stile at the end on to the road and turn left. As you walk along the road there is a good view of Peter's Stone and the valley below. Stay on this road which will take you back into the centre of Litton.

Walk 15
Miller's Dale

An attractive walk, which starts with some lovely stretches of the River Wye, through Miller's Dale and Chee Dale. It continues, with fine views on the way, to Chelmorton and the pretty village of Taddington, before crossing High Dale and returning along the Monsal Trail. Its ghostly interest lies in two stories at Taddington Hall and a strange wolf-like creature, which haunts the road back to Tideswell.

Distance: 9½ miles.

Grade: A/B.

Parking: Miller's Dale, Monsal Trail car park. From the A623 Baslow to Chapel-en-le-Frith road, turn on to the B6049 to Tideswell. After 3 miles and passing through Tideswell village, you pass under a bridge and past a Woodturning Supplies shop on the left. Take the next turn right, signposted Wormhill, P (Parking) and Toilets. Go up the hill, under the bridge and the car park is on the left.

Map Ref: SK137733. Outdoor Leisure 24 White Peak Area.

Pub Stop: The Church Inn, Chelmorton.

N.B. There are WCs situated on the old station platform.

Route

1. With your back to the WCs, turn right along the old station platform and continue to the far end, where the path curves to the left to the Monsal Trail. Cross straight over the Monsal Trail and bear left on to a footpath, with a sign at the end of it for Miller's Dale. Go along this narrow path, which goes through trees and then drops down some steep steps, with a handrail on the

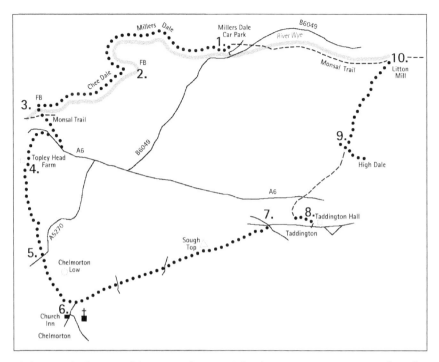

right. Just before reaching a road, turn right down two steps, situated to the right of a wooden gate, going right on to a broad path. Continue straight ahead on this path, which borders the River Wye, proceeding through Miller's Dale. Go under a viaduct and continue. The path becomes narrower and closer to the river but is most attractive, particularly in summer, with overhanging trees.

2. Pass a bridge on your left, and continue straight ahead on the right side of the river into Chee Dale. Note the warning concerning possible flooding, if the river is high. The path becomes rockier and climbs up and down by the river. You eventually come to a stile, with a sign to the left for Chee Dale. Turn left, over the little wooden bridge, and then continue with the river on your left. The path continues, meandering up and down, very rocky in places and inclined to be slippery in wet weather. Further on the path flattens and there is a high cliff to your left. The path becomes narrower again and passes under an overhanging cliff on your right. You then reach some stepping

stones, some of which are a long stride for short legs! They are also inclined to be submerged when the river is high, hence the warnings. (My least favourite part of the walk as I find some of them rather far apart and wet and slippery.)

After negotiating these you will come to a bridge, which you cross and then continue with the river on your right, passing a footpath to the left and heading for Wye Dale. Cross another bridge and continue now with the river on your left. You eventually reach a set of man-made stepping stones, which are much easier to negotiate. The path opens out a little, with steep cliffs on either side, enjoyed by rock climbers. Continue, passing under the bridge (Monsal Trail), going over a stile on the far side. On reaching the next bridge, climb the steps, but do not cross the river, but continue ahead still with the river on your left. You will eventually reach some cottages on the right-hand side. Turn left here over the wooden bridge.

3. On the far side of the bridge, turn almost immediately left, up a path situated to the left of the corrugated shed. The path climbs steeply uphill. At the top, just before the bridge, turn right through a gap in the wall dropping down and crossing the Monsal Trail. Go up the other side and over a stile, then go straight ahead. The path climbs steadily passing a footpath sign for 'A6 and Topley Pike lay-by'. On reaching a second footpath sign for 'Concessionary path Topley Pike lay-by', turn right and continue up to the road. Turn left on road and then almost immediately right at the sign for Topleyhead Farm. Go ahead on this paved road to the farm. Ignore a wooden stile on the left, then bearing round to the right towards the farmyard, go over a stone stile in the wall on the left, which is opposite the end wall of the farmhouse.

4. Bear right towards the dewpond, heading for an iron gate to be seen beyond it. The stile is to the left of the gate. Go ahead with a wall on your left. At the end of the field, go over the stile on the left, then turn right proceeding with wall on your right. Go over next stile, then bear left across the field, heading to the left of buildings to be seen ahead, to a stile in the top left-hand corner. Go over the stile and passing the buildings on your right, you will reach a water trough and an arrow sign. Turn right here and either climb the gate or climb on to the water trough and round the

gatepost. Follow the footpath marker and go down field to the bottom right-hand corner. Go over the stile and turn left and go straight across the lane and up a narrow path. Continue into a field, where you head diagonally across to a stile, situated to the right of a gate in the far end wall. Go straight across next field to reach the road.

5. Cross the road and go through gate on far side and cross the field with a wall on your right. Continue on a path, which contours round the hill to your left, which is Chelmorton Low. The path eventually drops down to a wooden gate, where you turn right down to a road and right again to the Church Inn, in Chelmorton.

6. Coming out of the pub, turn left up the hill and at the top, bear right on the bridleway. The path climbs steeply for a time, then flattens out, following the wall on your right. Note there are two paths, which run parallel across this area. Both come to a lane a few yards apart and both reach a bridleway sign, pointing back the way you came. Go on to the lane by either of these signs, where you turn right and then after a few yards, turn left over a stile in the wall. Head straight across the first field, to a stile in the wall, which is 30 yards to the right of an open gateway. Then in next three fields, follow the wall on your left, until you come to a muddy track, which you cross, bearing left to a stile. Cross seven fields, following the wall on your left. On entering the eighth field, where you see the reservoir ahead, bear slightly right to a stile to the right of the reservoir. (Sough Top Reservoir). Bear diagonally right in the next field, heading for a footpath sign and in same direction in following field. The path drops down the hill heading for the church steeple to be seen in the village of Taddington below. In the following field, follow the direction of the footpath sign as the path levels and then drops down to a lane. Cross the lane and continue down on the footpath. On reaching the bottom, go over a stile and down a path in between houses to the road. Cross the road to the main road where you turn right.

7. Continue down the village for about ½ mile, passing the Queen's Arms on the way until you reach Hall Lane and just beyond it, Taddington Hall, the last house on the left.

The Hall has two ghost stories associated with it. The first concerns a farmer, who was tending a sick mare on a snowy night in 1947. When the mare tried to bolt out of the stableyard, a voice from the gateway was heard, saying 'Whoa, Whoa'. When the farmer went to investigate who his helper had been, not only did he find no one but there were no footprints in the snow! The ghost was thought to be that of Isaac, who, with his brother, used to run a hessian factory in what is now the hall's saddle room. The brothers quarrelled and Isaac was found murdered, his brother having cut his throat. Since then Isaac is said to have haunted the hall.

Taddington Hall which has two ghostly tales attached to it.

The second story concerns a previous owner of the hall, who, every Monday, rode to Bakewell market and returned home rather inebriated. One Monday evening, his wife heard his horse return and saw her husband cross the yard in his usual tipsy state. The only difference was that his body then passed straight through the door without him opening it! A while later, some men arrived to say that her husband's body had been found at the bottom of Bakewell Hill. Since then, his ghost is said to haunt the hall on Mondays at twilight.

8. Go down Hall Lane, then turn left on bridleway. Stay on the bridleway, passing two fields on the right. At the end of the second field, turn right into the field and cross the field with a wall on your left. Go over a stile on to a lane where you turn right, continuing until you reach a dual carriageway. (A6). Cross over on to another lane. Go up this stony track, which becomes a green lane between walls. Pass a green lane to the left and continue until you cross another green lane, by a footpath marker, to a wooden gate. Cross five fields then you will come to a deep valley, which you need to cross. The actual footpath goes straight down, but as it is very steep you may find it better to go to the right for about 50-100 yards until you pick up a path climbing up from the valley below. Turn left down this path to the valley bottom (this is High Dale) then go up path on far side, bearing round to the right, passing between two hills.

9. After crossing a broken wall, cross two more fields, bearing left in the second to reach a stony lane, where you turn left and then right at the footpath sign. Go over the stile into the field and go straight up the field, following wall on your right to the top corner, where you go over the stile in left-hand wall. Turn right on the track and right again, keeping wall on your right, eventually bearing left to pass between a wall on your left and a fence on your right. Drop down to a stile in the right-hand fence. Cross stile and turn left down field. Cross a stile by the side of a wooden gate and continue down on a broad path, now veering away from the fence on your left. The path eventually reaches a stile at the bottom by the side of a footbridge. Turn right and go down the steps on to the Monsal Trail, where you turn left.

10. Stay on the Monsal Trail for 1½ miles. On the way, you pass a footpath to Priestcliffe, a bench for Bill Lester, Chappie's Log (who was Chappie?), a footpath to Miller's Dale, and a long bridge, passing over the River Wye and the road. Just after this, you will come to the station buildings on the right and the car park.

N.B. Opposite the entrance to the car park is a café called the Wriggly Tin Café.

Opening times Tuesday to Friday 12 to 5pm. Saturday and Sunday 10am to 6pm. (November to February, 10-5pm.)

Well worth a visit for teas, scones, home-made cakes and light meals. Wondering where its name came from? Its construction is the clue!

Take care if you are returning on the B6049 to the A6, particularly if night has fallen, for there are stories of cars being chased by a strange, wolf-like creature, which leaps and runs at great speed. Whether this creature is real or phantom is not clear, but the nearby village of Wormhill is where the last wolf in England was killed in the 16th century, which may have some bearing on these local tales.

Walk 16
White Lodge

This is a pleasant walk, which starts by following the River Wye, before climbing up Monsal Dale to Monsal Head, where there are wonderful views. It returns via Ashford-in-the-Water, then again along the River Wye.

It starts from an area still haunted by the ancient evil of Hulac Warren and the pure and beautiful shepherdess Hedessa. Later in the walk you see the 'house' of Hob Hurst, a giant with strange, mysterious powers. There is also an opportunity to visit the unusually named Infidels' Cemetery, an eerie haunted place.

Distance: 5¼ miles.

Grade: A.

Parking: White Lodge pay-and-display car park. This is situated on the A6, 2 miles from Ashford-in-the-Water, between Ashford and Taddington. The car park is on the left-hand side. WCs (albeit primitive ones!) are available in the car park.

Map Ref: SK171707. Outdoor Leisure White Peak Area.

Pub Stop: Monsal Head Hotel, plus Monsal View Café and Licensed Restaurant, at Monsal Head.

Route

1. In the car park, locate some steps, which are on the right, just past the pay-and-display unit. Go down these to the road (A6). Cross the road and go through the gap stile on the other side.

Across the valley, beyond the River Wye, the cliffs rise to the site of a prehistoric fortress, Fin Cop. It overlooks an area, which is renowned for an ancient legend involving the abduction and attempted rape of a beautiful shepherdess by an evil giant.

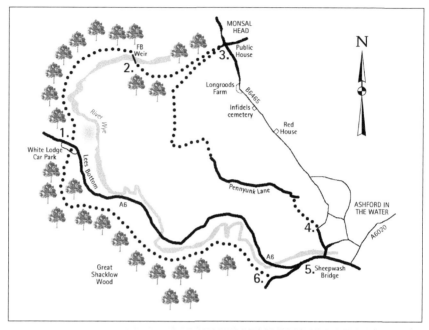

Hulac Warren, one of a race of giants, who lived in Demons Dale (Taddington Dale), desired Hedessa, a lovely shepherdess who was promised to another, and who resisted Hulac's advances. As she returned home one night, Hulac waylaid her and forcibly abducted her, carrying her to the top of the cliffs. Hedessa pleaded with him to release her but to no avail. She then cried out to the gods for help and, although they gave her the strength to free herself, in doing so she fell to her death in the valley below.

Hulac cursed the gods for interfering and in punishment he was turned to stone and stands forever as a rocky outcrop in the River Wye. It is said that where Hedessa fell, a spring of pure water appeared and her spirit still wanders this area. Villagers walking at night between Taddington and Ashford would cross the road to get as far as possible from the river and this place, which is haunted by ancient evil deeds.

Go straight down the field, crossing stream in bottom corner and go over the stile. Continue ahead on a path on the left-hand side of River Wye. At footpath sign, go to the right following the sign for Monsal Dale. The path meanders for about a mile until you reach a footbridge over the river.

2. Cross the river here and go ahead on a path, staying by the river past the weir, then continuing on as it climbs steadily up through woodland. On reaching some steps after ¾ mile, go up them to reach Monsal Head. There is the Monsal Head Hotel and also the Monsal View Café, a gift shop and ice cream shop.

3. After refreshments, go back down the steps you have just ascended, then after a few yards, take the footpath to Ashford (the higher of the two paths). The path climbs, goes over a stile, up some steps and then continues on the right-hand side of a wall with good views on both sides. A bit further on a wonderful view of Monsal Dale opens out.

Note the rocky outcrop on the hillside on the left-hand side of the dale, below the high headland. The rocky outcrop is known as Hob's House. The high headland is Fin Cop.

According to legend, Hob was a giant with strange mysterious powers, who was never seen by day. However, at night, if he liked you, he would come out and enter peoples' homes and do the work of ten men, thrashing their corn and completing their chores. However, if you upset him, by doing something as small as cutting down a tree on land he considered sacred, he could be very destructive and vindictive and could cause havoc. No wonder people would leave food and a bowl of cream on the hearth in the hope of placating him.

On the top of Fin Cop is the site of a prehistoric fortress. One must compliment the ancient warriors that built it on their choice, not only strategically, but also aesthetically for they looked out on a beautiful landscape.

On reaching a seat and footpath sign, keep to the left, following the sign for Ashford, going over a stile by the side of a wooden gate and into a green lane. Go over a stile by an iron gate, cross the next field and over a further stile into another green lane. Where the lane ends, go ahead across the field and then turn left before the iron gate, going into the field to your left and proceed down it with the wall on your right. On reaching the bottom corner, go over the stile by the side of an iron gate into another green lane. Continue on this lane for ¾ mile, and then watch for steps on the right, going up them to a stile and a footpath sign. Bear slightly to the right of the direction of the footpath sign, to pick up a footpath marker leading to a stile on the far side. Go over the stile and on to path between fence and wall. Go down steps and ahead.

4. On reaching the road, turn right then ahead, following the sign for Bakewell and Matlock and then go over the Sheepwash Bridge.

5. Turn right and cross road. Turn left at the sign for Sheldon, staying on this road until you reach a left-hand bend and a footpath sign, where you leave the road, to go ahead to a gate, with a gate stile at the side of it.

6. Having gone through the gate stile, go ahead on the lower right-hand path by the river. Stay on this path on the left side of the river. Where the river veers to the right, go straight ahead and on reaching a footpath sign, keep straight ahead again (i.e. not to the left). On reaching some buildings, with a bridge to the right, go on the path, which passes to the left of the buildings. Continue on this very pleasant path through trees, at first level and then climbing upwards for about ½ mile. Then go over a stile, over a wall. The path then starts to drop down and you leave the trees. A little further on you will come to a footpath sign, where you turn right. Go down this rocky path. On reaching a stile go over it and turn to the right, following the sign for White Lodge car park. Stay on this path back to the car park.

Point of Interest: Situated on the road from Monsal Head to Ashford-in-the-Water (B6465) is the 19th-century Infidels' Cemetery. So named because the gravestones make no reference to God and once thought to be for the burial of evil people and hence its reputation for being haunted. It is a small but eerie place, overgrown and with no public access, though it may be viewed through its front fence. It is said to be haunted by three ghosts, a vampire, a grey lady seen at dusk amongst the gravestones and a man in black, who is seen outside the entrance and then disconcertingly vanishes through the wall into the cemetery.

When I visited it with a friend, she felt a strong aversion, a feeling of being unwelcome and I, most unusually, had a nightmare the following night, where I felt a menacing presence, sitting on the bed behind me.

I have not included the Infidels' Cemetery in the walk, as the road is unsuitable for pedestrians, being both busy and narrow. However, avid ghost hunters may wish to visit it whilst in the area. It is situated about one mile from Ashford-in-the-Water, on the left-hand side, just after the Red House (on the right) and before Longroods Farm. If any one can throw any light on the origins of this strange isolated cemetery, I should be interested to hear from them.

Walk 17
Ashford-in-the-Water

A fairly easy 10-mile walk over the fields and through woods with good views, which takes in delightful stretches of both the River Lathkill and the River Wye. It has the strange tale of the Sheldon Duck and visits a 400-year-old haunted mine.

Distance: 10 miles.
Grade: B.
Parking: Small public car park in village and limited parking on village streets of Ashford-in-the-Water.
Map Ref: SK195678. Outdoor Leisure 24 White Peak Area.
Pub Stop: The Lathkill Hotel, Over Haddon.

Route

1. Go straight ahead out of car park. On reaching road, turn left and at end of the road, go over Sheepwash Bridge to the main road (A6).

Sheepwash Bridge was built in the 17th century and was a major crossing point of the River Wye for packhorse trains carrying malt from Derby.

The pen at the side was used for washing sheep to get rid of stones and soiling prior to shearing. The charge was 6d a score of sheep. (ie. 3p for 20 animals.)

Turn right and cross the road. Turn left at the sign for Sheldon, staying on the road until you reach a left-hand bend, where you leave the road, to go ahead to a gate, with a gate stile at the side of it.

2. Having gone through the stile, take the left-hand upper path, which

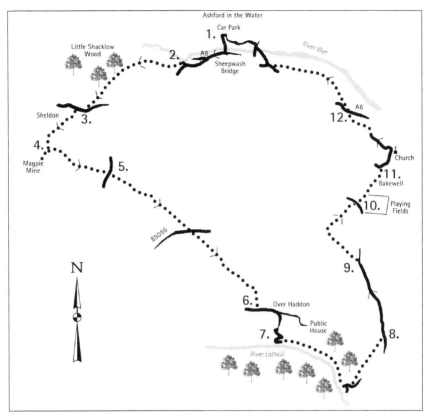

rises to a wall, where you turn left, following direction of the arrow sign. The path goes up by the wall on your right, before zigzagging round to reach another footpath marker. Continue ahead on this path, on the left side of a broken wall, towards the wood to be seen ahead. Continue on the left side of Little Shacklow Wood and at end of wood, go across the fields until reaching a stile on your left, go over it on to the road.

3. Turn right on the road, to the edge of the village of Sheldon to the 30mph speed limit sign.

Sheldon is an attractive village, which is mentioned in *Domesday Book*. Its population, which over the centuries has risen and fallen, owes much to the extensive lead mining in the area.

It has an interesting story dating back to the 17th century, when its villagers claim to have seen a duck disappear after flying up a tree. When the tree was later cut down, the wood had the outline of the duck ingrained within it. The wood was used in the timbered chimney breast of the oak room at Great Batch Hall in Ashford-in-the-Water and may still be seen there.

Then just after the 30mph speed limit sign at the top of the hill, turn left at the footpath sign. Go ahead on a broad track, through an iron gate and continue straight ahead with wall on your right for three fields. Then go over the stile into fourth field, with wall now on your left. Turn left at the footpath sign and head diagonally across the field towards The Magpie Mine to be seen ahead. The Magpie Mine is a good place for a coffee stop.

The Magpie Mine was worked for some 300 years from the early 17th century. Its workings show examples of lead mining over a long period, from its square Derbyshire pumping house chimney and later round Cornish chimney, its engine house and chimney which date from the early to mid-18th century, to the steel headgear and winding engine which belong to the 1950s.

The mine is said to have been cursed by the widows of three miners killed in the early 19th century, in a dispute with rival miners over a lead-bearing vein. Certainly, since that time, the mine has had a history of floods, fires and roof falls.

One of a party of geologists, exploring the mine in the 1940s, reported seeing a man carrying a candle, who suddenly disappeared where the tunnel ended. The apparition was dismissed as imagination, until the photographs from the mine were developed and showed that one of the members, standing on a raft in a flooded sough, was accompanied by a second figure, standing on top of eight feet of water! Was he guarding his claim or trying to show them where to find a rich vein of ore?

4. Standing by the round chimney, with your back to the mine, head for the round structure and bear right to the corner. Go over the stile and turn right, and then ahead, with the wall on your right, to a footpath sign, where

The Magpie mine, at Sheldon, which is said to be cursed.

you turn right through stile in the wall. Bear left across next field to corner of wall, then continue with wall on your left. A broad path continues between two walls until you reach a road.

5. Cross the road, go over the stile opposite and straight up the field. At the top, go between walls to a stile by a gateway. Go over the stile and turn right and over next stile. Bear left across the field to finger post and continue in same direction. Go over the stile and turn left with trees on your left. Go to the bottom of the field and a footpath sign, where you turn right across bottom of field. Go over a stile and diagonally across next three fields in same direction, continuing to the road.

Cross the road and turn right and over the stile, following the direction of footpath sign, diagonally crossing two fields. Go over the stile into third field, then halfway along, go over the stile in the wall on the left. Bear slightly right across next field, heading to 2 o'clock, to a stile in the wall to the right of the two gateways. Go over the stile and diagonally across next two fields (heading in direction of Over Haddon to be seen ahead). In second field, head for the stile that is to the left of the open gateway. Go over the stile and down next field, with the wall on your right, crossing stile at the bottom on to the road.

6. Turn left into Over Haddon. The pub is located at the other end of the village.

If you are visiting the pub, keep straight ahead on the main road. On reaching a T-junction, turn right and then left to the Lathkill Hotel. On leaving the pub, turn right. Then at the next junction, go straight ahead on the minor road. At the next T-junction, turn left past the Yew Tree Tea Rooms and go down the lane.

If you do not wish to visit the pub, turn first right on entering Over Haddon, at the sign for 'Parking'. The lane drops down past a public car park, with WCs and picnic tables. As an alternative to the pub, there are the aforementioned Yew Tree Tea Rooms, on the opposite side to the car park, which is reputed to be friendly to walkers.

Continue down the lane as it winds down the hill to the river.

7. Turn left and, with the river on your right, follow the path as it rises to give lovely views of the River Lathkill below. In times of drought it sometimes disappears underground on the first part of this path, reappearing further on. There are some beautiful blue and green pools to be seen – a most attractive walk.

Continue until you reach the road, where you turn left up the hill. After a right-hand bend and parking area, continue for about 50 yards up the hill, watching for a gap stile in the wall in the hedge on the left. Turn left through the stile and up to the field. Keep straight ahead across a very large field, to a stile, which is in the middle of the wall, at the end of the field i.e. not through gateway. Go straight across next field to the road.

8. Turn left on road and stay on it for ¼ mile, passing Noton Barn Farm and a road to the left to Over Haddon. Ignore footpath to the right, then after another ½ mile, following a right-hand bend, where road starts to drop down into a dip, go through stile in the wall on the left.

9. Bear diagonally right across the field to the stile to the left of gap in the wall, across next small field and then ahead with wall on your right. Go through stile by wall, then at end of next field, turn right by hedge to bottom corner. Go over the stile and left, then right down side of hedge, with hedge on the left. Through stile and ahead again, passing a school on your right until you reach the road.

10. Go straight over road on to public footpath between playing fields. At end, take left-hand path where paths fork. Continue ahead on road between houses. The path drops steadily down heading towards Bakewell Church, passing between attractive gardens. Then down some steps to a road.

11. Turn left and on reaching the Monyash Road, turn right. Just before the church, bear left up a narrow road, passing church on your right. Where a road joins from the right, go ahead, slightly left, to where you can see a sign for Fly Hill and Youth Hostel. Stay on this road as it bends to the right, then just past St Anselms Preparatory School, turn right at the footpath sign for Ashford. Bear left to another footpath sign and cross playing field at bottom of steep bank to a third footpath sign and a track into the wood. The path drops steeply down to the road.

12. Cross the road and turn left, then after a short distance, turn right through stile by the gate. Cross the field on to path between wall and fence, then cross the road and continue on narrow fenced path. Then go ahead on a well-defined path, which runs parallel to the river, with spectacular views of the weirs along the way. Stay on this path until you see a footpath sign leading you back on to the road. Turn right and right again over the bridge and keep straight ahead. On reaching the main road, cross over and bear right on to the road into the village.

Note the old iron milepost by the bus shelter 'LONDON 154', which shows Ashford was on a Turnpike. This type of milepost only had LONDON cast on them. The other names and distances had to be painted on.

Follow the road round to the left and note that on the left-hand side is Great Batch Hall.

This was where, you will recall, the timbered chimney breast, bearing the imprint of the duck, is situated. Great Batch Hall is also reputed to have a ghost, albeit a benign one!

A little further on, turn right up Court Lane, passing the Church on your left and reaching the car park on your right.

Walk 18
Bakewell

A fairly easy seven-mile walk starting from the town of Bakewell, with its 17th and 18th-century houses, interesting shops and of course, Bakewell Puddings. The walk is on good paths, starting on an old packhorse route and has attractive open views.

It passes the Hassop Estate, which had a prophetic talking beech tree. In the latter part of the walk, you may (or may not!) wish to visit Shady Lane to meet a ghostly funeral cortège.

Distance: 7 miles.

Grade: A/B.

Parking: From the Matlock side of Bakewell, go through Bakewell and on the A619 go over the River Wye bridge. Turn first right and right again into the pay-and-display car park.

Map Ref: SK221686. Outdoor Leisure 24 White Peak Area.

Pub Stop: The Packhorse Inn, Little Longstone, ⅔rds of way through walk.

The Saxons and the Romans were attracted to Bakewell because of its warm springs. Its Saxon name, 'bad quell' meant bath well.

Route

1. Leave the car park by the exit at the far end i.e. the opposite end to the vehicle entrance. Go straight across the road and through a small iron gate, signposted 'Scot's Garden'. Go on to a path on the right-hand side of the river. The path follows the side of the river and then veers away to the right towards a wall. Go through two wooden gates, then follow the path, on the right-hand side of the river, then bearing right to a third wooden gate in the wall leading on to a road.

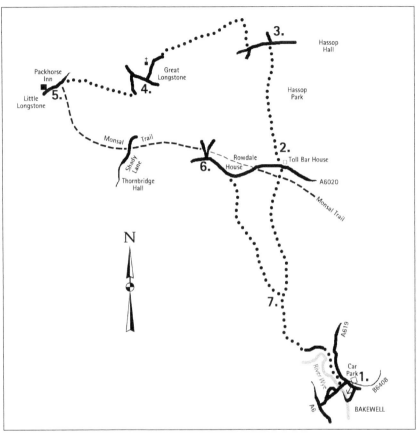

Turn left on the road, then turn right on a stony lane, signposted 'To The Monsal Trail'. Continue to climb up this stony paved lane, passing an old tunnel on the right. You will also pass The Packhorse Forge on the right.

This path was an important packhorse way and some of the original paving can still be seen.

Go through an iron gate and continue ahead on the stony track across a more open grassy area. Where the track goes to the left through two broken walls, leave the track and go ahead across the grass to a stile by an iron gate, with a dew pond to the left.

Continue straight ahead, still on the packhorse way, on a broad grassy track between two walls. The path continues first between walls and then on the left side of a wall for about I mile, reverting to walls on either side on the latter part. The path eventually drops down through a wooden gate and on to the Monsal Trail. Cross straight over, through a second wooden gate marked 'Public Bridleway'. Go straight across the field to the rather charming building called Toll Bar House.

This was where the packhorse way you have been following, crossed the turnpike road from Buxton through Ashford-in-the-Water. A private road was built from Edensor by the Duke of Devonshire to link up with the Buxton/Ashford turnpike and then later the whole road was adopted as a turnpike.

2. On reaching the road, turn left and turn right at next footpath sign. Go over the stile and straight ahead, heading for a small copse of trees behind a wall. On reaching a high wall, continue along it, with the wall on your right, for about ½ mile. Where the end of the wall drops lower, go over a stile in the wall and turn left, again following the wall on the right, until you reach a road. This wall borders Hassop Park.

To the right is the Hassop Estate, the ownership of which was in dispute for many years. In the grounds of Hassop Hall, there was said to be a prophetic, talking beech tree, which stood in front of the mansion. When the wind came exactly from the west, it was said to murmur 'All hail, true heir, that stills my voice' or some say 'All hail the Eyre, that stills my voice' a reference to the Eyre family. It was said that anyone attempting to hack down the beech tree met with an accident and it was thought that, buried beneath the tree, were documents which would be discovered by the person at whose hand the tree was felled, presumably the rightful heir.

3. On reaching the road, turn left and continue until you reach a road on the left. On the opposite side of the road, there is a narrow track, adjacent to a road sign for Great Longstone and Rowland and Hassop. Turn right on

to this track, which has a wall on the right. At the end of this track, go through a gateway and turn left, to go through a stile in the wall to the left of the barn. Cross the fields, then go straight over a green lane (Handrake Lane). Cross three more fields leading on to another green lane. On reaching a stony lane, turn left and then turn right at the road, going past the Church to the main road.

4. Turn right and go up Main Street to the War Memorial on the left. Turn left up Station Road between the War Memorial and the Crispin pub.

Turn right at the footpath sign and follow path across five fields. In fifth field bear right slightly, heading for buildings to be seen ahead. On reaching the road, turn left to the Packhorse Inn at Little Longstone.

5. Coming out of the pub, turn left, going back down the road. Turn right at the sign for Ashford and the Monsal Trail. Go ahead over two fields, then by the side of a wall to a stile in the wall. Turn left on the Monsal Trail. On reaching some buildings on the right, pause to consider whether you wish to take the following (very short) diversion, particularly if it is nearly twilight.

Shady Lane, near Thornbridge Hall, where a funeral cortege of 12 headless men may be seen.

Just before the railway bridge, turn left up the steps and at the top, turn right over the bridge and continue for about 100 yards down Shady Lane to the ornate gates of Thornbridge Hall. On a dark day or when nearing twilight, this lane, which is overhung with trees, is an eerie place with an eerie reputation. For here, it is said that, at twilight, may be seen a procession of 12 headless men carrying an empty coffin. They will not greet you or indeed pay you any attention, but one must ask, for whom is the empty coffin intended? Could it be for the unfortunate rambler who meets this strange procession?

Return to the Monsal Trail and your route then continues under the railway bridge on the Monsal Trail for about another ½ mile. Where the trail goes over a bridge, crossing a main road below, go left down a steep path, situated on the left, on the far side of the bridge, to reach the road.

6. Turn left on road and go under the bridge. Bear left at fork marked 'Baslow' and on to the main road (A6020). When you reach some buildings on the left, (Rowdale House) turn right through a stile in the wall and ahead across the field, contouring round the slope to the right, then heading for a gate to be seen ahead. Go through gate and up, on a very pleasant path on the edge of the woodland.

On reaching a stile, go over it and to the right across a grassy field, heading for the left-hand side of a wood and to a kissing gate to the left of a building. Continue in the same direction across the next field, then, when you see the spire of Bakewell Church ahead, go through stile in the wall on your left. Turn right, following the path as it bears slightly left. On reaching the dew pond, go over the stile to the left of the iron gate.

7. From this point you are retracing your route from the start of the walk. Go ahead down the grassy slope, on to a stony track and through an iron gate. Stay on the stony path until you reach the road, where you turn left. Turn right through gate stile and head for the river. Go through two wooden gates and continue ahead, eventually reaching the road. Cross the road and back into the car park.

Walk 19
Rowsley 1

A fairly easy walk, in pleasant undulating countryside, full of ancient history dating back 4,000 years and an abundance of ghostly interest.

It starts from Rowsley, which takes part in the well dressings. Three wells are dressed, plus there is the Rowsley Festival the last weekend in June.

Distance: 10 miles.

Grade: A/B.

Parking: Turn off A6 at Rowsley, on minor road opposite Peacock Hotel, signposted 'Stanton in Peak, Caudwell's Mill and Craft Centre'. After right-hand bend, park on roadside adjacent to playing fields. WCs are available at Caudwell's Mill and Working Craft Museum, which is also worth a visit for the Mill, craft shops and possibly refreshments at the end of the walk.

Map Ref: SK256656. Outdoor Leisure 24 White Peak Map.

Pub Stop: Red Lion pub or Druid Inn, Birchover.

Route

1. Return to the corner and turn right at the footpath sign for Stanton Lees. Go up this track for about 1¼ miles. Turn right at the footpath sign for Stanton Lees and go up the hill with a wall on the left. Go through a gate on to a lane. After passing Stanton Woodhouse Farm, continue ahead on a broad track. After a stone gateway, follow direction of footpath sign, bearing left, then passing the disused Endcliffe Quarry on the left, continue to the road.

2. Turn right and then turn left up a road marked Stanton in Peak, and then left on to the footpath. Follow direction of footpath sign up the field. In the woody knoll, take path to the right and continue ahead with a wall

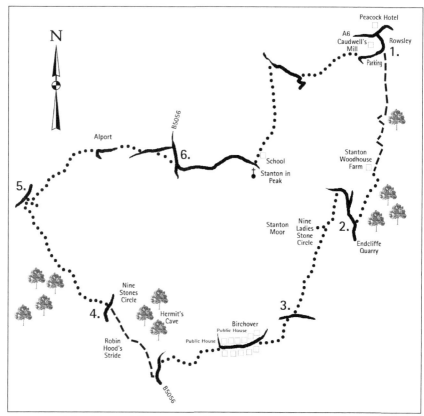

on your right. Turn right over a stile, crossing a broad track to reach the Nine Ladies Circle.

This plateau has been in use since 2000BC. This stone circle is 35 feet in diameter and 130 feet to the south west of it is the King Stone (also known as the Fiddler's Chair). According to legend, the Devil played his fiddle for nine ladies dancing on the Sabbath and so infuriated God that he turned the ladies to stone for disregarding his holy day.

A ghostly male figure, all in black, has often been seen standing just outside the circle, but there is no clue as to his identity. Perhaps it is the devil viewing the scene of his 'crime'?

Modern day witches still meet on Stanton Moor and report a strong feeling of evil in the area of Nine Ladies Circle. There are many tales of strange lights and experiences on the moor, including abduction by a UFO and also the report of a ghost of a white lady.

Earl Grey Monument, which lies about 300 yards to the south west, on the edge of the moor, is said to be haunted by a spectral black dog, with flaming eyes, huge teeth and a foaming mouth! Not wishing to meet that one, we shall take a different route, heading south west and hope that it doesn't roam far from its haunting grounds!

Return to the broad track and turn right. Stay on this track, going straight on where paths cross, continuing to the road.

3. Turn right on the road, then left on the footpath. Follow wall on the left, heading down to farm. In farmyard, bear left following direction of arrow. Turn right following footpath sign. Where public footpaths cross, turn right through stile in the wall. Continue on the lane until you reach the road. Turn left continuing into Birchover. There are public WCs on the right and the Red Lion pub. Continue through village, heading for the lane to the left of The Druid Inn.

Before proceeding down this lane, you may wish to pause at the Druid Inn, which is renowned for its good food. It also has the ghost of an old lady, with a very warm and caring smile, reported to have been seen sitting in the corner of one of the small downstairs rooms.

Also, behind the inn, are Rowtor Rocks, thought to have been used by Druids in the past, which have a longstanding reputation for being haunted by malevolent spirits. A cloaked ghostly figure is the most frequent apparition, although it is said that, on moonlit nights, others may be heard weeping and wailing at passing travellers.

The Revd Thomas Eyre used the natural rock formations and by carving armchairs, alcoves and staircases, created a retreat with fantastic views over the surrounding area. Below the rocks is the Jesus chapel, with some remarkable carvings created out of 22 different kinds of wood, the work of a previous vicar and a shortage of wood in World War Two.

At the eastern edge of the rocks there was a huge 50-ton 'rocking stone', which could be rocked by one hand until a group of youths toppled it in 1799. Although replaced in position, its balance could not be restored. It seems that vandalism is not just a 20th-century disease!

Rowtor rocks, near Birchover, haunted by malevolent spirits.

Returning to the lane, go past the Church, then left at a footpath just past a pond, going up the field. Turn left on stony track. Go through stile to the left of iron gate and turn right. Continue ahead on this path, eventually dropping down to a track and bearing right and immediately left over the stile, down path to the road. (B5056). Turn left, then right on the lane and immediately right over the stile to the left of iron gate (marked 'Private Drive Footpath only'). Go up broad track then follow direction of footpath sign across the field up to Robin Hood's Stride, the rocky outcrop to be seen ahead.

This is also known as Mock Beggar's Hall as the pinnacles resemble chimneys. Just behind the main rocks, in the shadow of an ancient yew tree, there is a cave named Cratcliffe Hermitage, which is believed to have been used by several hermits over the centuries. It is also said to be haunted by a monk.

This area abounds in stone circles, burial mounds and other remnants of an ancient era and is rich in local stories, being haunted by a white lady, a headless horseman, a green man plus there are numerous reports of lights hovering in the sky.

Robin Hood's Stride, also known as Mock Beggar's Hall, an area of many ghostly sightings.

Continue straight ahead, then turn left over the stile and immediately right over another stile, going diagonally left across the next two fields to the road.

If you look to the right, two fields away, there is another stone circle, Nine Stones Circle, that is Bronze Age. There is no public access to this circle, which is the focus of many of the stories. Unfortunately, only four of the stones now remain, though a nearby the gatepost may be a clue to the fate of the rest!

4. Go straight over road, and follow sign 'Public Footpath to Youlgreave'. Follow footpath signs around farm. Continue ahead, taking care to follow

footpath signs and markers, then dropping down field, going through a gate stile, then bearing right on a broad path. Follow path around hill to the left, then turn right at standing stone and stile, heading towards the village of Youlgreave. Continue straight ahead for five fields. In the 6th, turn right through stile ⅔rds of way along wall on the right and bear left across next field to the road.

5. Turn right, then after the crossing river, turn right on public footpath. Continue ahead on a broad path, winding by the River Bradford. Bear left through a stile (where lane goes up the hill) to keep river on your left. Continue to the road in Alport (by telephone box.). Turn right and immediately right again down the road. Then turn right over the bridge over the river, then left up path to the road. Turn left on road, then straight ahead at the left-hand bend, past Bank House on a short lane, continuing on to a path. Ignore stile to the right and keep ahead past caravan park and a field. In following field, bear right to the stile in the wall, going into next caravan park and continuing in same direction across the grass between the vans to the road.

6. Turn left and immediately right on minor road, and go up the hill, signposted 'Stanton in Peak'. Continue climbing up this road, ignoring footpath to Hawleys Bridge and continue into Stanton in Peak. Just before the church, turn left on the footpath, going past school and continuing through iron gate and straight ahead following wall on the left across the field, then in same direction across next field, heading for trees. Continue past wood and then follow waymark across three fields and ahead in same direction in fourth large field. In fifth field, head for the bottom right-hand corner, dropping down the hill. Continue in same direction in sixth field, over the stile to the left of gateway on to lane (Stantonhall Lane). Turn right up the road, then left at the footpath sign at Dove House Farm. Go through stile at side of gate and follow track round to the right, down into dip and up other side, then in next field, bear slightly right, towards a line of trees, to join a broad grassy track. Continue on this track to the road and ahead back to cars.

Walk 20
Rowsley 2

This is a shortened version of Walk 19. It is a fairly easy walk, in pleasant undulating countryside, visiting Stanton Moor, which has been in use since 2000 BC. Although short, this walk has plenty of ghostly interest.

It starts from Rowsley, which takes part in the well dressings. Three wells are dressed, plus there is the Rowsley Festival the last weekend in June.

Distance: 4 miles.

Grade: A.

Parking: Turn off A6 at Rowsley, on minor road opposite Peacock Hotel, signposted 'Stanton in Peak, Caudwell's Mill and Craft Centre'. After right-hand bend, park on roadside adjacent to playing fields. WCs are available at Caudwell's Mill and Working Craft Museum, which is also worth a visit for the Mill, craft shops and possibly refreshments at the end of the walk.

Map Ref: SK256656. Outdoor Leisure 24 White Peak Map.

Pub Stop: None but refreshments available at Caudwell's Mill.

Route

1. Return to the corner and turn right at the footpath sign for Stanton Lees. Go up this track for about 1¼ miles. Turn right at the footpath sign and go up the hill, with a wall on the left. Go through a gate on to a lane. After passing Stanton Woodhouse Farm, continue ahead on a broad track. After a stone gateway, follow direction of footpath sign, bearing left, then passing disued Endcliffe Quarry on the left, continue to the road.

2. Turn right and then turn left up a road marked Stanton in Peak, and then left on to the footpath. Follow direction of footpath sign up the field. In the woody knoll, take path to the right and continue ahead with a wall

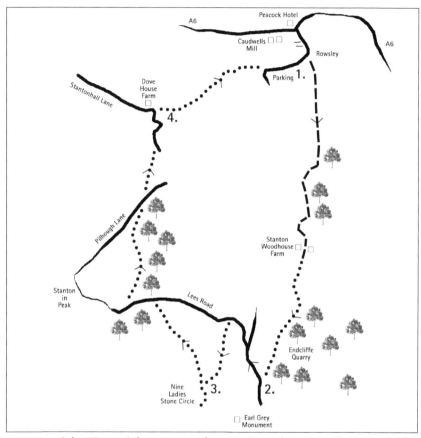

on your right. Turn right over a stile, crossing a broad track to reach the Nine Ladies Circle.

This plateau has been in use since about 2000 BC. This stone circle is 35 feet in diameter and 130 feet to the south west of it is the King Stone (also known as the Fiddler's Chair). According to legend, the Devil played his fiddle for nine ladies dancing on the Sabbath and so infuriated God that he turned the ladies to stone for disregarding his holy day.

A ghostly male figure, all in black, has often been seen standing just outside the circle, but there is no clue as to his identity. Perhaps it is the devil viewing the scene of his 'crime'?

Nine Ladies Stone Circle, Stanton Moor.

Modern day witches still meet on Stanton Moor and report a strong feeling of evil in the area of Nine Ladies Circle. There are many tales of strange lights and experiences on the moor, including abduction by a UFO and also the report of a ghost of a white lady.

The appearance of so many ghostly white ladies may have something to do with the ancient practice of sacrificing a young virgin, in order to placate the various earth and water gods worshipped by our ancestors.

Earl Grey Monument, which is about 300 yards to the south-west, is said to be haunted by a spectral black dog, with flaming eyes, huge teeth and a foaming mouth! Not wishing to meet that one, we shall take a different route and head north-east, and hope that it doesn't roam far from its haunting grounds!

3. Return to the broad track and turn left and continue on this path until you reach a road. Turn left and continue along the road until you reach a footpath on the right. Go down this footpath on the edge of the wood until you reach another road. Turn right and then left at the footpath sign. Go

down steps and continue in same direction across two fields (one large one, where walls have been removed, and the following one) to reach another road. Turn left down the road, then after two Z-bends, turn right at Dove House Farm.

4. Go through stile at side of gate and follow track round to the right, down into dip and up other side. Then in next field, bear slightly right, towards a line of trees, to join a broad grassy track. Continue on this track to a road and then go ahead back to the parking place.

Walk 21
Darley Dale

An easy 9-mile walk from Darley Dale to Winster, taking in the attractive Clough Wood, which is magnificent in May time when it is awash with bluebells. The walk is full of points of historical and ghostly interest and returns over the majestic sweep of Wensley Dale

Distance: 9 Miles.

Grade: A.

Parking: Take B5057 off A6 at Darley Dale. Go past Railway Station and continue to the left-hand bend. Park in picnic area car park on the right. (There are WC's at the Railway Station.)

Map Ref: SK270623 Outdoor Leisure 24 White Peak Area.

Pub Stop: Miners' Standard Inn, Winster.

Route

1. Turn right out of car park, to Darley Bridge. Go over the bridge and bear right, then turn right, signposted Stanton Lees. The road climbs steadily. Ignore two footpaths to the left. Where the road forks, go left on to lane (Oldfield Lane). Near the top of the hill, where there is a broad track to the left, bear left on to it and go through a gap by an iron gate. When the path divides, take the right-hand, higher path, going past the folly. Continue through Clough Wood on a very pleasant path, which can be wonderful at bluebell time as the slopes are covered. Your woodland path continues for about ¾ mile and then starts to climb. At the top of the hill, go over a stile and ahead on a broad grassy track. Go over the next stile on to a stony lane.

2. Turn left on to Clough Lane.

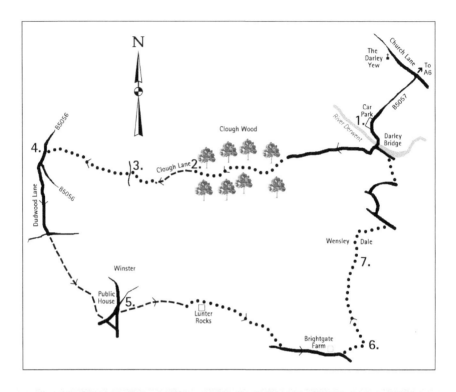

Clough Lane is an old packhorse way, which would have been paved by the local parish. Some of the old gritstone paving can still be seen. It was most likely used for transporting ore from the local lead mines. This would be carried in two baskets, one on either side of the saddle, each basket being about 10ins wide, 20ins long and 30ins deep and the load could weigh as much as 2½ cwt.

Continue on this lane, ignoring footpath signs to the right and left to Birchover and Winster. Continue past farm (Upper Town Farm). Ignore stile to the left just after farm. Stay on the lane until you reach the road in Upper Town.

Note the old stocks on the opposite side of the road. You could be put in the stocks for such misdemeanours as using foul language, drinking instead of attending church services, gambling on the Sabbath and whilst there, would be pelted with rotted refuse by the local villagers.

3. Turn left then right on to another footpath. Go ahead on this broad cart track, continuing across two fields with fence/hedge on your left. Then go on to a narrow path, through a wooded area. Where the path opens out again, this is a nice place for a coffee stop. Bear right towards the wall, continue with wall on your right past buildings and ahead. The path continues past a ruined building, then through a gate stile. It drops down to a broad track, where you turn right then immediately sharp left over a stile on to a path dropping steeply down to the road below (B5056).

4. Turn left along road, then turn right on to lane and then take the lane to the left (the left one of three). This is Dudwood Lane (Limestone Way).

Dudwood Lane is part of an ancient Iron Age north/south route through Derbyshire, which, even in Saxon times was known as the 'Old' Portway. A portway, originally, was a way to a market town.

There is a long steady climb for ½ mile until you reach a main road. Go over the road, bearing slightly left on to a stony lane (Islington Lane).

As your way continues on Islington Lane, the 17th-century Portway lead mine (named after this route) is to your left. The Portway mine became one of the richest in Derbyshire, in the 18th century, producing over £60,000 worth of lead ore between 1746 and 1753. Islington Lane is the only reminder of the village of Islington, which grew up around the mine but had disappeared by the 19th century.

Cross the next road reached after ½ mile and continue ahead until you reach the next road. Turn left and then left again at the B5056 to the Miner's Standard Inn.

A standard was a dish in which lead ore was measured. The initials over the door, E.P.E.P.F.P. don't stand for Every Person Entering Pays For A Pint as

has been suggested, but for Edith, Ella and Frank Prince, together with the date the Inn was built, 1673.

The pub is reputed to be haunted. Footsteps have been heard in one of the upper rooms and a woman's voice humming the first three notes of the nursery rhyme *Three Blind Mice.* Perhaps she was singing her children to sleep?

The Miners Standard Inn, Winster, where a ghost of a woman singing nursery rhymes may be heard.

5. Turn right out of the pub and go up the road to a structure on the right called a Lead Ore House – a sort of night safe for Lead Ore, then cross the road to the footpath opposite marked 'Limestone Way' and continue on this track. After ¾ mile, cross a stile by an iron gate and go ahead. After reaching an open gateway, bear slightly left, following arrow sign, keeping to the left of a dew pond and go ahead in the same direction, following the line of a broken wall on your right to pass under Lunter Rocks, a rocky outcrop to the right.

A murder took place in a house, which originally perched upon Lunter Rocks and the rocks are said to be haunted due to this. There are also tales of strange dancing lights called 'will o' the wisp' or the not so nice name of 'corpse candle' said by some to foretell death. I understand the village children won't play here in the late evening.

Go over a stile in a wall and straight ahead on a well-defined path. Go through another stone stile, staying on the left of the wall, until you reach a stile where you cross to the right-hand side of the wall. Continue ahead with the wall on your left for two more fields, then the path bears right crossing three more fields. Cross a broad cart track and go straight ahead to a stile. In the following field, the path goes diagonally right to the road. Turn left. Ignore footpath to the right and further on ignore footpath left at Tearsall Farm. You will reach Brightgate Farm and a pillar-box and on the next bend, a footpath sign to the left. Go through the stile by the gate and turn right. Go straight ahead across first field.

6. At the end of the second field, turn left following the line of the path coming in from your right and heading for a mast on the skyline. Try to keep in line with this mast and follow this line down into the valley. The path here is indistinct. You will eventually reach a stile in the bottom left-hand corner. Continue to another stile, turn right to a finger post (i.e. not on the cart track) and continue down in the same direction (i.e. away from the cart track which goes to the left across the field). When you reach a field with a ruined building in the right-hand top corner, bear right down to the bottom of this field.

7. Drop down steeply and cross Wensley Dale and go through stile on far side, then halfway across next field, turn right to the stile in middle of the wall. Bear left across next field, through stile to the left of gateway. Follow direction of arrow, and heading for fingerpost, (to the left of farm) continue up to the road. Turn left, then right on to minor road, signposted Darley Bridge. The lane drops down the hill. Ignore the footpath sign to the right, then just past the houses, turn right down Flint Lane. The lane drops and continues along until just before some more buildings, there is a stile to the left. Go over this stile and straight ahead over next stile and continue in same direction over last field to a track. Turn left and then right over the bridge.

Darley Bridge was an ancient crossing of the River Derwent. It has two of its original arches, which are pointed. The original bridge had seven arches according to a 17th-century reference to it.

Continue along the road back to the car park.

The Darley Yew and Darley Church situated on the former Ghost Lane.

Worth a visit: If you are returning to the A6, before you pass the railway station, the road to the left is Church Lane. In the 17th century it was known as Ghost Lane, the ghost being that of a Scottish pedlar, who was robbed and murdered there. His ghost is seen near the large sycamore tree 150 yards from the churchyard. At the other end of the lane, lies Darley Dale Church. In the churchyard is one of the largest yew trees in England, said to be over 2,000 years old, although some sources say it may be only 1,000. Whichever it is, its trunk is an amazing sight and well worth a visit. Around its base are commemorative tablets, depicting some of the most important battles of World War Two, erected soon after each event took place.

Walk 22
Youlgreave

An attractive, scenic walk, taking in three dales. Bradford Dale which has rocky, tree-clad sides and beautiful still pools of water and clear streams, Gratton Dale, a pretty steep-sided dale, with a stream trickling through it and Longdale, which is more open and wilder. The lovely scenery along with headless ghosts, phantom coaches and a ghostly duel should make it a walk to remember.

Distance: 9 miles.

Grade: B.

Parking: From the main road in Youlgreave, almost opposite the Bull's Head pub, take the narrow road behind the large round structure, past the tiny Thimble Hall Cottage and turn right on to Moor Lane. Continue for about a mile and you will come to a car park on your left. Park here.

Map Ref: SK194655. Outdoor Leisure 24 White Peak Area.

Pub Stop: The Duke of York, Elton.

Youlgreave is the only village in Derbyshire to have its own water authority. The large round structure (where you turned off Church Street, opposite the Bull's Head) is known locally as the Fountain and was built to supply Youlgreave's water in 1829.

Youlgreave also takes part in the Derbyshire well dressings. Five wells are dressed and this annual event begins on the Saturday nearest to 24 June.

Route

1. Take the footpath at the back of the car park on the left and go down this path which is part of the Limestone Way, continuing down the fields to the

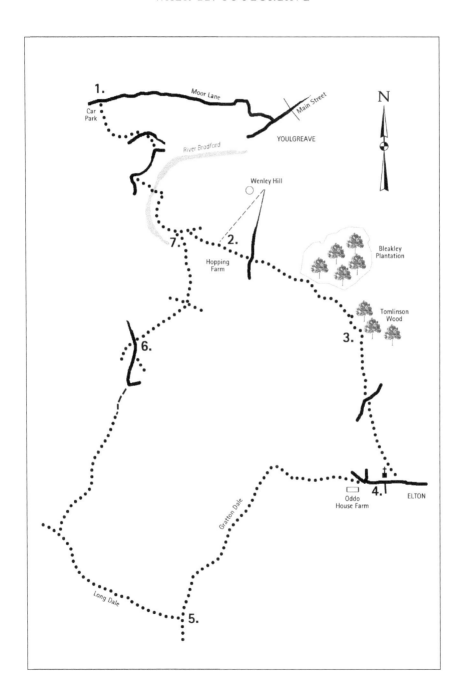

road. When you reach the road, turn left and then right on to the footpath again. At the next road turn right.

On this road which runs between Youlgreave and Middleton, a phantom coach and horses have been seen, lit by ghostly lamps and accompanied by ghostly dogs. One witness is said to have felt the wind of its passing!

Go left on to the footpath at the next corner, through a gap in the wall. The path then zigzags down to Bradford Dale. Cross over the bridge to the far side of the Dale and turn right and continue along this path. Where the path bears round to the right, passing a sheepfold, and forks, take the left-hand path and continue ahead. A little further on, you climb up some steel steps to a path above, where you turn right and continue ahead, keeping the stream on your right (not crossing stream).

But, before you proceed, check the height of the river over the stepping stones to your right, as this is your return route. Now go ahead, and where the path forks, take the right-hand path, crossing a stile and continuing straight ahead to the right of a mound and through buildings, to a track, which you cross.

The track to the left leads to Wenley Hill. One day, two brothers were walking up this lane to Wenley Hill, when a man appeared and walked ahead of them, but then suddenly vanished before their eyes. Not only that, but the brothers both agreed that he had no head! Other strange tales from Wenley Hill include a sighting of a headless dog and that it is said that no birds sing there. I must say there was not a twitter when I visited it!

Why are so many ghosts headless? Of course, it may be that they are the ghosts of persons who died by being beheaded, either accidentally or murdered/executed. Does the suddenness of death by beheading affect the spirit so that it cannot accept that it is dead? Or does the trauma of being beheaded imprint itself on the fabric of time? Another theory suggests it is to do with the ancient practice of decapitating corpses and placing the head between the knees for burial. Whatever the reason there does seem to be a lot of them!

Wenley Hill, where no birds sing.

Go on to a footpath into a field.

2. Continue on the footpath up the field with wall on the left, through two stiles and then turn right continuing up the hill with wall on the right to the road. Go straight over and over the stile opposite, climbing steeply uphill for two fields, (there are excellent views to the left at this point) heading for the right-hand corner of Bleakley Plantation. Ignore the path which crosses your own and keep straight ahead across next field, then bear diagonally right over next two fields. Follow the wall on your right in the following field then, at the footpath sign, go diagonally right in the next, heading for Tomlinson Wood. Crossing into the next field, turn left towards wood and then go to the right-hand side of Tomlinson Wood.

3. Turning right at the footpath sign across the field, continue on this path to a farm track, over the stile, and across the fields bearing slightly left to the stile in second. Go over it into the next field, then following wall on the left for a short distance, look for a stile in the wall and go left here to the road.

Go straight over the road and up the path to Elton, turning right past the church to the crossroads, to the pub opposite called The Duke of York. This pub is one of the few in Derbyshire to appear on CAMRA's national inventory of exceptional interiors.

4. Coming out of the pub, turn left and go along road to where the roads fork (two to the right). Go straight ahead on a footpath to the right of Oddo House Farm, then following a wall on the right, go down field to footpath sign. Turn right following the sign 'Public Footpath to Gratton'. Going on to a track, follow it round to a sign for 'Limekiln', where you turn left through a gate along Gratton Dale, a pretty steep sided dale with a stream running through it.

5. After about a mile you will come to a gate, which you go through and then turn right into Longdale. After about another mile, go through a gate in a wall on the left and turn right. Then take the grassy track bearing right up the hill. At the top, go through the gap in the wall on the right and continue, following wall on the right, across the fields until you reach a track. Continue straight ahead. After about ¼ mile, bear left down through iron gate, down narrow track between stone walls to the road, where you go straight on.

6. Take the **second** footpath to the right, opposite a track and footpath sign, climbing up the grassy slope and then bearing left along the top of the valley. The path drops down and goes through a stile in the wall, where you turn right. Keep straight ahead and cross a track, continuing across the fields, eventually reaching the River Bradford. Cross the river by the stepping stones and turn left.

7. From here you are retracing your route from the first part of the walk. Continue along Bradford Dale, descending by the steel steps and following the path ahead. Ignore the path to the left and keep ahead to where it bears round to the right and continues along the right-hand side of the dale. When you reach the bridge, turn left over it, to ascend the zigzag path to the road at the top. Turn right and (watching out for phantom coaches, particularly if it is now twilight!), where the road bends right, take the footpath left uphill. At the next road turn left, then go right on to the footpath, climbing steadily up the path back to the car park.

The Old Hall, Youlgreave, where a Roundhead and a Cavalier remain locked in immortal combat.

The Old Hall at Youlgreave has a haunted Duel Room, where on a dark November night, a re-enactment of a fatal duel between a Roundhead and a Cavalier may be seen, the ghostly figures forever locked in immortal combat. The Old Hall is situated on Church Street (the main street through Youlgreave) at the bottom of Moor Lane (your road to and from the car park).

Walk 23
Alsop-en-le-Dale
Station 1

An easy 9¼-mile walk from Alsop-en-le-Dale Station, which travels through some beautiful scenery. You travel north through Wolfscote Dale, following the River Dove, before swinging back south to Alstonefield and your pub stop at The George. The latter part of the walk includes the lovely Hall Dale before returning to the River Dove and climbing up Nabs Dale. The walk finishes with a visit to the site of a gruesome 500-year-old murder, whose ghostly sounds may still be heard.

Distance: 9¼ miles
Grade: A/B.
Parking: On A515 Ashbourne to Buxton Road. At a point approximately 5½ miles from Ashbourne (or 15½ miles from Buxton) there is a sign for Parking and Alsop-en-le-Dale Station on the right-hand side from Ashbourne. Turn in here and park in pay-and-display car park, which is adjacent to the Tissington Trail.
Map Ref: SK155549. Outdoor Leisure 24 White Peak Area.
Pub Stop: The George, Alstonefield.

Route

1. Go on to the Tissington Trail, which runs alongside the car park, heading north i.e. up the trail near where you entered the car park, signposted 'Hartington 5 miles Parsley Hay 7 miles'. Go past the first footpath to the left, reached after ¼ mile and continue for a further ½ mile, until just before a bridge, take the next footpath on the left, which drops down the hill. Go over the stile, then through the gate to the left, with a sign 'Bradburys Bank'. Then bear left across the field following footpath marker post. Cross first field to a gap in the wall and continue in second field, again following a

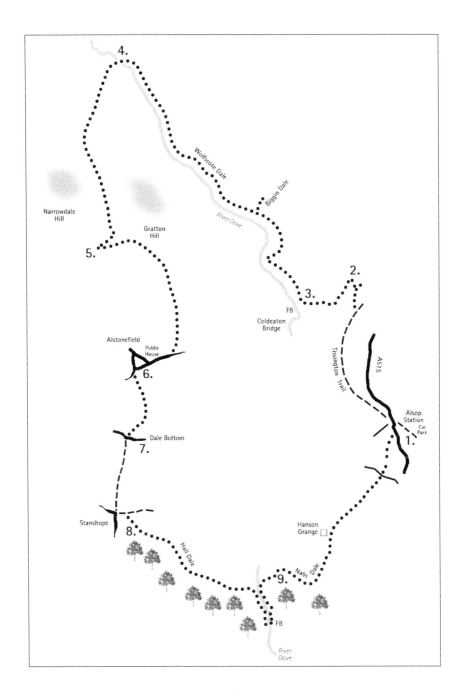

footpath marker. The path travels parallel to the dale below. There is a lovely view of the dale at this point. Continue to another footpath marker, gradually dropping down to the dale below.

2. On reaching the dale, turn left and continue down the dale with a wall on your right. The path drops down through an attractive steep sided dale. Go over a stile and continue down. On reaching the bottom of the dale, where you meet another path crossing your own at the side of the river, turn right, going through the stile at the side of a wooden gate. A few yards further on you will come to a footbridge, which is known as Coldeaton Bridge.

3. Keep straight on past the bridge and continue along this broad path with the River Dove on your left. After ½ mile, you will pass some stepping stones on the left followed by a stile. The hill across the river from the stepping stones is known as Gypsy Bank. Continue straight ahead in this very pretty dale. After about another 300 yards, you will reach a stile and a junction where Biggin Dale comes in from the right. Your way continues straight ahead in Wolfscote Dale, which is attractive with rocky limestone outcrops. Continue ahead for 1¼ miles. When you reach the end of the dale (there is a sign on the left for the start of Wolfscote Dale and a cave in the hillside to the right), go through a gap stile and left over a footbridge over the Dove.

4. After crossing bridge turn right and continue ahead with the river on your right. After about 100 yards, you go through a gap stile and the path veers away from the river and continues with a wall on your right. Go through a wooden gate and then turn left on a broad track. Continue straight ahead, crossing a stile by a gate a little further on and through two iron gates, still following a wall on your right. Where the lane turns to the right, go straight ahead to the side of an iron gate and into a narrow grassy dale. Stay on the path in the bottom of the dale. After going through an iron gate, go straight on to a wall, then go ahead on to a path with the wall on your right. Go over the stile by another iron gate and continue ahead. Where the wall ends, go straight on, moving now to the right side of a wall. The path starts to rise and at the top, on reaching a stone wall ahead, turn right by a wire fence and go over a stile into a green lane. There is a good view

looking back over your route at this point, with Narrowdale Hill on the left and Gratton Hill on the right.

5. After passing an iron gate on the left where the track bends to the right, continue for about 100 yards, to a footpath sign where you turn left and immediately left again, going ahead with the wall on your left. Continue ahead following arrow signs. Go to the left of the corner of the wall i.e. not through the gateway. Go through next gateway and across a small field to a gap stile and gate by an arrow post. Go straight across next field to a stile on the far side. Go through another gate and gap stile and across another two fields, through stiles at sides of iron gates. Continue ahead in following field, heading for marker post. Go over the stile into a green lane and turn right. Ignore footpath sign to the right and keep straight ahead on this lane, passing a lane to Gypsy Bank on your left, continuing until you reach a road. Turn right and follow the road into Alstonefield and the George pub on the village green. (There is also a tea room around the corner.)

6. On leaving the pub turn right and then right again. Pass a road joining from the right and then, at the next junction, turn left and then immediately left again, passing a cottage on your right and going on to a green lane. On reaching a junction of paths, follow the sign 'Public Bridleway to Stanshope', going through a stile at the side of a gate and down the field with the wall on your right. Follow wall as it bends to the right, then over a stile and continue to follow the wall as it drops down to Dale Bottom.

7. On reaching a road, cross over and go up the track on the far side. Note there is a lovely cottage with a very pretty cottage garden to the right on the road. Go up the track as it climbs steeply at first and then levels out and continues for ¼ mile, going on to a lane and passing Grove Farm on your left. You will eventually reach a road, where you turn left and immediately left again down a stony lane. After about 100 yards, turn right through a gap stile with a (broken) sign for Dovedale. Cross first field and go over a stile and then in same direction over next field. Following arrow signs, go straight ahead with a wall on your right.

8. Go over step stile then a wooden gate stile and continue down into Hall Dale, a very attractive steep sided dale. Hall Dale is ¾ mile long, the upper part being grassy and the path becoming rockier on the lower part. On

reaching the River Dove, turn right through a stile in the wall and continue along the side of the river until you reach a footbridge. Cross the river and turn left on the far side, walking with the river now on your left. Continue for ½ mile until, just after some large caverns, turn right on a path marked 'Alsop-en-le-Dale 1¾ miles'.

9. This stony path climbs quite steeply through shrubs and trees for ½ mile. On reaching the top of Nabs Dale, go over the stile into a field, which is a good place for a break opposite Hanson Grange.

The hauntings in the area of Hanson Grange may date back to 1467, when four men murdered John Mycock there. John de la Pole of Hartington, struck him on the side of the head, Henry Vigurs of Monyash stabbed him in the breast, Mathew Blands of Hartington hit him with a staff and John Harrison shot him in the back with an arrow. No reason is given for the murder but they were summoned to appear before the King in 1469 but failed to turn up. They certainly were determined to 'do him in' and it must have been a dreadful attack. It is said that if you are near Hanson Grange, particularly in autumn, you may hear the sound of the murder being committed. Some people have reported hearing a man pleading for his life to be spared, whilst others report the sound of men fighting.

The eerie sounds may have an even longer history as the name Hanson comes from Hans Syn Dune, Hill of High Sin. This suggests previous bad deeds and may date back to the times when the Saxons and Danes fought for control of the land.

Proceed ahead to the footpath sign and turn left following sign for Alsop-en-le-Dale. Go over the stile at side of farmyard gateway, then bear right up the hill, going to the left of the telegraph post, to a stile in the wall. Follow direction of footpath sign to a farm track, where you turn right. On reaching a signpost, follow sign for Alsop-en-le-Dale and continue on a paved track, later passing New Hanson Grange. On reaching a minor road go straight over and over the stile in the wall. In field go ahead to the right of wood, to a stile in the wall leading on to a main road (A515). Cross over and on to the track back to car park.

Walk 24
Alsop-en-le-Dale
Station 2

An easy six-mile walk from Alsop-en-le-Dale Station (a shorter version of walk 23), which travels through some beautiful scenery. From the Tissington Trail, you descend through a very pretty dale to reach the River Dove at Coldeaton Bridge. After crossing the river, there is a short but steep ascent, continuing on level paths to Alstonefield and your pub stop at The George. The latter part of the walk includes the lovely Hall Dale before returning to the River Dove and climbing up Nabs Dale, at the top of which, you may hear the ghostly sounds of a 500-year-old murder!

Distance:	6 miles.
Grade:	A/B.
Parking:	On A515 Ashbourne to Buxton Road. At a point approximately 5½ miles from Ashbourne (or 15½ miles from Buxton) there is a sign for 'Parking and Alsop-en-le-Dale Station' on the right-hand side from Ashbourne. Turn in here and park in pay-and-display car park, which is adjacent to the Tissington Trail.
Map Ref:	SK155549. Outdoor Leisure 24 White Peak Area.
Pub Stop:	The George, Alstonefield.

Route

1. Go on to the Tissington Trail, which runs alongside the car park, heading north i.e. up the trail near where you entered the car park, signposted 'Hartington 5 miles Parsley Hay 7 miles'. Go past the first footpath to the left, reached after ¼ mile and continue for a further half-mile, until just before a bridge, take the next footpath on the left, which drops down the hill. Go over the stile, then through the gate to the left with a sign 'Bradbury's Bank'. Then bear left across the field, following footpath marker post. Cross

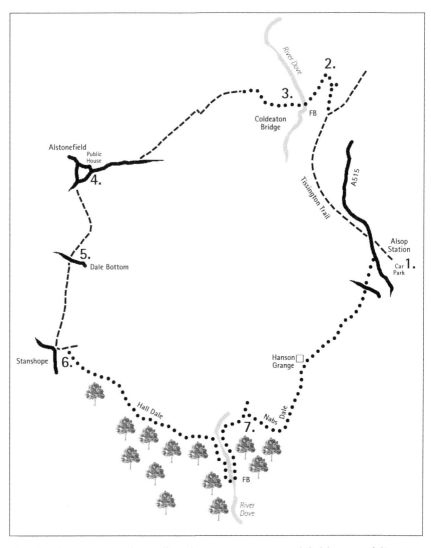

first field to a gap in the wall and continue in second field, again following a footpath marker. The path travels parallel to the dale below. There is a lovely view of the dale at this point. Continue to another footpath marker, gradually dropping down to the dale below.

2. On reaching the dale, turn left and continue down the dale with a wall

on your right. The path drops down through an attractive steep sided dale. Go over a stile and continue down. On reaching the bottom of the dale, where you meet another path crossing your own at the side of the river, turn right, going through the stile at the side of a wooden gate. A few yards further on you will come to a footbridge, which is known as Coldeaton Bridge.

3. Cross the bridge and go straight up the hill, heading for the gap between the two hills to be seen ahead. The path climbs steeply for about 300 yards, reaching a stile at the top. Go over the stile on to a green lane and continue between walls for about ¾ mile until you reach a road. Turn right and continue on the road into Alstonefield and the George pub. (There is also a tearoom around the corner.)

4. On leaving the pub, turn right and then right again. Pass a road joining from the right and then, at the next junction, turn left and then immediately left again, passing a cottage on your right and going on to a green lane. On reaching a junction of paths, follow the sign 'Public Bridleway to Stanshope', going through a stile at the side of a gate and down the field with the wall on your right. Follow wall as it bends to the right, then over a stile and continue to follow the wall as it drops down to Dale Bottom.

5. On reaching a road, cross over and go up the track on the far side. Note there is a lovely cottage with a very pretty cottage garden to the right on the road. Go up the track as it climbs steeply at first and then levels out and continues for ¼ mile, going on to a lane and passing Grove Farm on your left. You will eventually reach a road, where you turn left and immediately left again down a stony lane. After about 100 yards, turn right through a gap stile with a (broken) sign for Dovedale. Cross the first field and go over a stile and then in same direction over next field. Following arrow signs, go straight ahead, with a wall on your right.

6. Go over a step stile, then a wooden gate stile and continue down into Hall Dale, a very attractive steep sided dale. Hall Dale is ¾ mile long, the upper part being grassy and the path becoming rockier on the lower part. On reaching the River Dove, turn right through a stile in the wall and continue along the side of the river until you reach a footbridge. Cross the river and turn left on the far side, walking with the river now on your left.

Hanson Grange. The area is haunted by a 500-year-old bloody murder.

Continue for ½ mile until, just after some large caverns, turn right on a path marked 'Alsop en le Dale 1¾ miles'.

7. This stony path climbs quite steeply through shrubs and trees for a half-mile. On reaching the top of Nabs Dale, go over the stile into the field, which is a good place for a break opposite Hanson Grange.

The hauntings in the area of Hanson Grange may date back to 1467, when John Mycock was murdered there by four men. John de la Pole of Hartington struck him on the side of the head, Henry Vigurs of Monyash stabbed him in the breast, Mathew Blands of Hartington hit him with a staff and John Harrison shot him in the back with an arrow. No reason is given for the murder but they were summoned to appear before the King in 1469 but failed to turn up. They certainly were determined to 'do him in' and it must have been a dreadful attack. It is said that if you are near Hanson Grange, particularly in Autumn, you may hear the sound of the murder being committed. Some people have reported hearing a man

pleading for his life to be spared, whilst others report the sound of men fighting.

The eerie sounds may have an even longer history as the name Hanson comes from Hans Syn Dune, Hill of High Sin. This suggests previous bad deeds and may date back to the times when the Saxons and Danes fought for control of the land.

Proceed ahead to the footpath sign and turn left, following sign for Alsop-en-le-Dale. Go over the stile at the side of the farmyard gateway, then bear right up the hill, going to the left of the telegraph post, to a stile in the wall. Follow direction of footpath sign to a farm track, where you turn right. On reaching a signpost, follow sign for Alsop-en-le-Dale and continue on a paved track, later passing New Hanson Grange. On reaching a minor road, go straight over and over the stile in the wall. In the field, go ahead to the right of the wood, to a stile in the wall, leading on to a main road (A515). Cross over and on to the track back to the car park.

Walk 25
Hartington

Starting from the delightful and interesting village of Hartington, this is a fairly easy walk with good views of the Upper Dove Valley. Your route follows an ancient packhorse route and calls at the Packhorse Inn at Crowdecote. The return route passes Pilsbury Castle, a Motte and Bailey Norman fortification. If you are thinking of spending the night at Hartington Hall Youth Hostel, it may be a restless one due to its ghostly occupant.

Distance: 8½ miles.

Grade: A.

Parking: Either park in centre of Hartington or from the centre, take the B5054 Warslow Road to a public pay-and-display car park on the right-hand side. WCs are available on opposite side of road from car park.

Map Ref: SK128605 Outdoor Leisure 24 White Peak area.

Pub Stop: The Packhorse Inn, Crowdecote.

For those of you who like staying at Youth Hostels, Hartington Hall is one with a difference and you can have your ghost without walking a yard! It said to be haunted by a young servant girl, who wanders from bed to bed, peering at the occupants. Several people have woken to find her bending over them. She is said to be looking for her lost love, Bonnie Prince Charlie. He, supposedly, stayed at the hall and having fallen in love with the servant girl, promised to return one day. Unfortunately, he never did, and she is said to have died of a broken heart and now endlessly wanders the house and garden, still seeking her prince. The Hall is situated on Hall Bank, which is on the left as you enter Hartington on the B5054 from the A515.

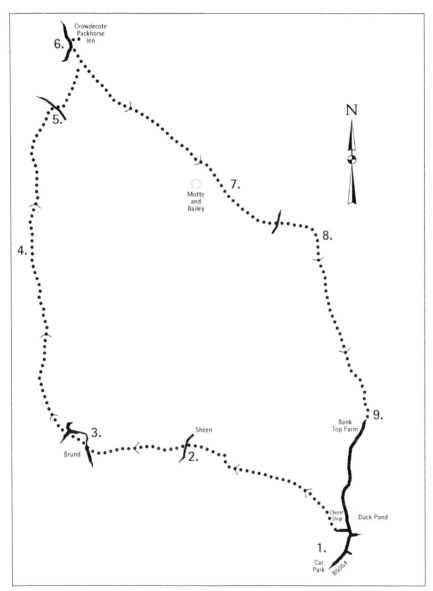

Route

1. From the duck pond in the centre of Hartington, go down lane at the side of the Cheese Shop (which is well worth a visit). Turn right over the stile at

the footpath sign, ahead over the field, and through wooded copse. Then on to path and continue ahead across three fields. In next field, go ahead, but bear slightly left, (but not going on to broad track to the left) then dropping down into the dip and bearing right to bridge over stream.

Go up the field to the stile by iron gate, over lane and continue ahead, following the sign for Sheen, climbing steeply up the hill on a broad track. Go over the field at top and ahead for two more fields, dropping down and crossing two further fields into a dip. Go over a stile and up the next field, heading between the farm on the right and the cottage to its left, to reach a stile on to the road at Sheen.

Sheen was mentioned in *Domesday Book* and was on an ancient packhorse route, known as a Saltway. From the 17th century on, salt was transported from the brine pits of Cheshire to markets in Derbyshire and Nottinghamshire. The path you have travelled from Hartington is thought to be part of a packhorse route that continued to Matlock Bridge and your way continues on the packhorse route to Brund.

Sheen is also famous for its tug-of-war team, which has achieved success in National, European and World Championships.

2. Turn left and then right over the stile at waymark marked 'Public Footpath to Brund'. Go straight ahead across four fields on to a green lane, staying on the lane as it bends to the right and continuing down to a tarmacked lane in Brund. Turn right and then left at the footpath sign and follow direction of arrow across the field. Cross stream and on to another lane, where you turn right. Bear round to the left and immediately left again at the footpath sign.

3. Go over next stile then follow wall on the right. Go straight ahead through the trees and continue to a stile on the left. Cross into next field and continue again with wall on the right. Over next stile and ahead over a very muddy area (always muddy!) then bearing right following direction of arrow on post, heading across the field. Continue across four fields, and in the fourth, go to the left of the barn, over stream and ahead. Going by another barn, cross next field, then a green lane and ahead across three more

The village of Hartington, where the hall is haunted by a broken hearted maiden.

fields. Then in the fourth bear right over a stile in the wall, before reaching a barn. Cross two stiles (together) and a boggy area/tiny stream, then ahead in field, passing to the left of the farm. Go through a stile into a field, and then pass a footpath sign, following its direction to Longnor, staying on the left side of the wall.

4. In second field after footpath sign, head for buildings in the top right-hand corner, going over the stile to the right of buildings. Go straight ahead through buildings and ahead through iron gate (not left down the track) and straight on again at the footpath sign. In next field, go to the left of barn. Continue following fence/wall on the right. At tumbledown barn, bear right to the stile in the corner, where there is a signpost 'footpath to Crowdecote'. Pass to the right of buildings and straight ahead to the top right-hand corner of field. Continue over next field to the road.

5. There are excellent views to the left of the Upper Dove Valley, with Chrome Hill and Parkhouse Hill dominating the landscape. (Chrome is pronounced 'Croom' and is from the Old English 'Crumb' meaning curved or sickle-shaped).

Turn right on road and left through stile, then to the right following direction of footpath sign and arrow post to drop down the hill. At the bottom of the slope at the wall, turn left to the stile. Go straight ahead down field to the right of the trees, over the bridge and turn left on the lane to Packhorse Inn at Crowdecote.

The name Crowdecote derives from Cruda's Cot. Cruda would be a Saxon landowner and Cot, a cottage or shelter.
The Packhorse Inn is an attractive, old-fashioned pub, which is welcoming to walkers. However, in packhorse days the inn was the cottage in front of the present pub.
Packhorses generally travelled in 'trains' of 40 or 50, each bearing a saddle with rows of brass bells on it. As the packhorse ways were too narrow for two trains to pass, it was necessary to give warning – hence the bells.
The packhorse route from Bakewell and Monyash to Longnor crossed the River Dove by the bridge at Crowdecote.

6. Coming out of the pub, turn left back on to the lane, but continue straight ahead, past the bridge you crossed on the right, continuing on a broad track. Keep straight ahead across three fields, and then climb the hill, round the mound of Pilsbury Castle.

This is a motte and bailey Norman fortification. Motte = mound forming a site for a castle. Bailey = the outer wall of a castle.

Just past the mound, go over a stile on the left and bear left up the hill, following wall on the left.

7. Go over a stile at the top of the rise and continue straight ahead, still with wall on your left. Go over a stile to the left of an iron gate and ahead across two more fields, following direction of arrow. Over a lane and follow footpath sign for Hartington. Head towards wall ahead, and then bear right up the hill to the stile in the top right-hand corner.

8. Go over the stile and straight ahead, heading for waymark post at corner of wall (not through gap halfway along). Continue to follow

direction of arrow ahead across remainder of field. On reaching the corner of the walls, turn left, heading for the gateway, with a stile at the side of it, to be seen ahead. Next, head for wide gap in the wall ahead, and then bear right to 2 o'clock, to a stile near the right-hand corner. Continue ahead on a broad grassy path. Go over two more stiles and through a gap in the wall. Then continue straight ahead, following the blue path markers, joining a wall on your left and eventually reaching a lane, where you turn right dropping down to some farm buildings.

9. Turn left and continue ahead on this lane, which will lead you eventually back to the duck pond at Hartington.

Walk 26
Spend Lane, near
Ashbourne

This is a pleasant, easy walk over the fields and on the tracks, in this area to the east of Dovedale. There is the opportunity to visit Tissington Hall and the walk finishes with a ghostly lane.

Distance: 3½ miles.

Grade: A.

Parking: Take the A515 Ashbourne to Buxton road. About one mile from Ashbourne, turn left at a sign for Thorpe, Ilam and Dovedale. Continue to a millstone sign telling you that you are entering the Peak District National Park. Then ½ mile past this sign, where you come to a junction, where the main road turns left, turn right (signposted Tissington) and immediately left into a car park called Narlows Lane.

Map Ref: SK163505. Outdoor Leisure 24 White Peak Map.

Pub Stop: Dog and Partridge pub by parking area available at beginning and end of walk.

Tissington takes part in the Derbyshire well dressings. Six wells are dressed and the festival lasts for a week starting from Ascension Day (usually in May depending on Easter). To check Tel: 01335 352200.

Route

1. Come out of the car park and turn left. Then go right on to a minor road with a sign for parking on the corner. Go down this road and just before a gateway turn left at a public footpath sign. This path goes under a bridge, which is the Tissington Trail. Go down to a gate stile at the bottom. Cross over the stone bridge and bear right to another gate stile at the side of an

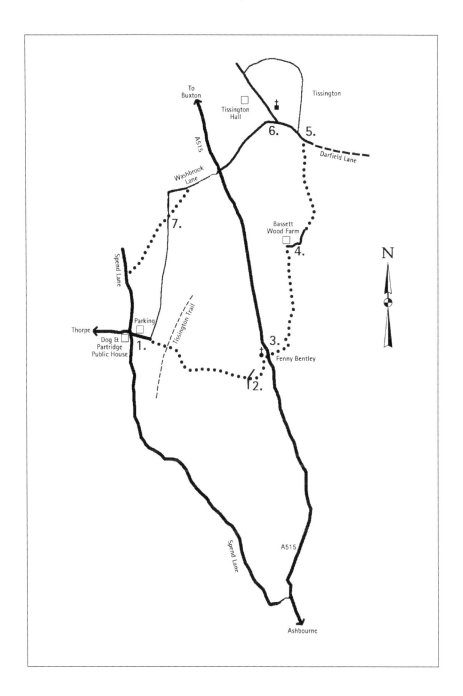

iron gate, signposted Fenny Bentley. Follow the direction of the sign up the field. On reaching another gate stile at the top, go through it and up the field with a hedge on your right. On the far side of the field, go through another gate stile and continue straight ahead, dropping down a long field, to reach an iron gate at the bottom. Continue downwards to a lane.

2. Cross the lane and go into the field. Go straight ahead, then at the end of the fencing of the first house on the left, turn left to a stile in the corner. Go past a building on your right and straight ahead to the churchyard. Bear right in the churchyard, eventually reaching the lychgate and the main road (A515), in Fenny Bentley.

3. Turn to the right on the road and cross over. Then just past the telephone box, turn left at the public footpath sign for Tissington. The path veers to the right past a lovely ornamental bridge and through a stile by an iron gate. Just past the last house on the left, bear left, cutting across a corner of this field, to where another field juts into this one. Stay in the same field, keeping to the right of the hedge i.e. not through the gateway. Go up the field keeping the hedge on your left. Nearer the top, bear right to the top right-hand corner of this narrow part of the field. Go over the stile and following the direction of the arrow sign, go up this field and the next one with the hedge on your left. At the end of the second field, bear right to a gateway, then across the following field, heading to the right of the farm buildings (Bassett Wood Farm).

4. Go over the stile by the side of a gate and then right on a farm track. Stay on this track until, about 50 yards after a sign for a 'Trekking Centre', you reach a stile in the hedge on the left. Go left over this stile. Go ahead across this field with a hedge on your left, then through a gap stile on the far side. Bear diagonally right across the next field, heading eventually just to the left of the farm buildings. Go over the stile and turn left on to a broad track/lane.

5. Go straight ahead on this lane (Darfield Lane) which crosses over the Tissington Trail, then passes a pond. A little further on, you reach the school and a road to the right. Your route lies straight ahead.

However, you may wish to make a short diversion here on the road to the right, to the very attractive Tissington Church and further on up the road Tissington Hall.

Spend Lane, north of Ashbourne, the scene of many unexplained incidents.

Tissington Hall was built in 1609 and has been the home of the FitzHerbert family for over 400 years. The ninth baronet, Sir Richard FitzHerbert (the capital H of Herbert distinguishes this branch of the family from those in Staffordshire), lives at the hall with his wife Lady Caroline and their two children. The Hall and Gardens may be visited at specified times in the summer. (For details Tel: 01335 352200). Sir Richard, who conducts the guided tours of the hall himself, could not tell me of any ghostly stories connected with the hall. Perhaps, as most ghost stories seem to arise out of tragedy, the hall has always been a very happy home,

The Old Coach House Tea Rooms are well worth a visit and are open throughout the year, though with more limited opening from October to December. For details Tel: 01335 350501.

6. Continue up this road for half-a-mile, until you reach the A515 Ashbourne to Buxton Road. Cross straight over on to the minor road opposite, signposted Thorpe and Dovedale. Go down this lane (Washbrook Lane) until, 50 yards past a barn, at the bottom of the hill, go left through a gap stile by a public footpath sign. Follow the direction of the sign across the field, then go through a gap stile on the far side.

7. Then go across a lane and through the stile on the other side. Follow the direction of the footpath sign across the next five fields. In the last field, the stile is 50 yards to the left of the buildings. Go on to the lane and turn left.

This is Spend Lane and is the scene of a number of unexplained incidents. In 1977, the occupant of a car was driving along it, when the car was filled with a tremendous wind, even though the windows were all shut. There was the sound of upholstery ripping, though later, the only damage found was that a metal disc had been torn off the dashboard.

In another incident on the lane, a girl had been thrown by a normally well-behaved horse.

In 1955, the car carrying a party of wedding guests crashed into a ditch on Spend Lane, just at the time the top tier fell off the wedding cake at the reception!

The lane is also known as an accident blackspot, with many accidents happening there.

There is a local story dating back several hundred years that a bride, travelling from Fenny Bentley to her wedding in Ashbourne, was tragically killed when her carriage turned over and this tragedy happened in Spend Lane and is perhaps connected with these later incidents.

There are good views of Thorpe Cloud to the right. Stay on this lane all the way back to the junction, where you turn left back into the car park.

Take care if you are travelling back to the A515 to Ashbourne, as you will still be on Spend Lane and its junction with the A515 must be one of the worst in Derbyshire!

Walk 27
Ilam 1

Starting from Ilam, a very attractive village with its Alpine style houses, this 10-mile walk takes you to Wetton, with superb views of the Dove Valley on the way. It returns through pleasant valleys and woodlands. On your route, you may meet a phantom coach and horses and later, you may look forward to encountering a horse with its headless rider.

Distance: 10 miles.
Grade: B.
Parking: On the main street of Ilam or in the car park attached to Ilam Hall.
Map Ref: SK136508. Outdoor Leisure 24 White Peak Area.
Pub Stop: Ye Olde Royal Oak, Wetton.

Ilam Hall is haunted by a 'White Lady' who has the habit of waking up people who are staying in the Youth Hostel, so if this is your base for walking you may be in for a sleepless night! She is also seen wandering the corridors and between the Church and the Italian Garden.

A phantom coach and horses is also said to be seen turning around in one of the old courtyards. Phantom coaches are usually black, pulled by headless horses with a driver with skeletal or grotesque features. They are often driven at a furious pace and are thought to be seen prior to a death in the family.

Route
1. From the centre of Ilam village, go up Orchard View, then turn left over a stile and ahead on a broad track through the park. Where the track turns left, bear right to the left of the railed grassy area/pond. On reaching a stony

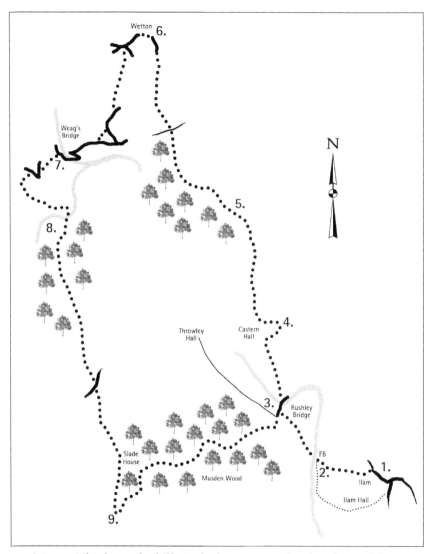

track turn right down the hill. At the bottom, go ahead and turn left over a footbridge over the River Dove.

2. Cross the first field to the stile, then bear right, cutting across the corner of the next field. Continue in the same direction across next field on a broad grassy track. Go ahead parallel to the wall on your right to another stile by

A White Lady may wake you up when visiting Ilam Hall.

a gate and cross next field. Then follow direction of finger post down next field to the stile to the right of the buildings. Go ahead by fence to lane.

The lane opposite, which leads to Throwley, is said to be haunted by a phantom coach known as the Cromwell Coach. In the daytime, only the sound of its wheels may be heard, but at night, its lights may be seen. Is this connected to the one seen turning round in Ilam Hall? It is said that anyone who gets in the way of such phantom coaches will be carried away to their doom!

3. So to avoid being mown down by phantom coaches, we shall turn right down the road, cross Rushley Bridge, then turn immediately left through stile in the wall. Bear right across the field, heading to the left of barns to be seen in following field. N.B. Stile is to the left of gateway. Continue in same direction in next field, heading for the top corner. Go ahead up the hill through trees, heading for the woody knoll, and a lane. Turn left and almost immediately right up some stony steps. Follow the wall on your right, then

go through a stile. Continue to follow the wall on your right, heading to the right of the buildings (Castern Hall).

Castern Hall – the history of the building dates back to the early 11th century and the house was restored during the reign of William and Mary. One of Derbyshire's oldest families, the Hurt family, occupied it from the 15th century. It passed out of their family before World War Two, but was bought back by them a few years ago. It is said to be haunted by a 'benign' ghost.

Join a track, then following a small footpath sign by the wall of the hall, go ahead on a lane following it round to the back of the hall.

4. Go over cattle grid and then follow footpath sign and go straight ahead with wall on your left i.e. leaving lane. Go on to a broad cart track. N.B. There are good views of the Dove Valley below. Continue with the wall on your left for two long fields. Go over the stile by the gate and then bear

Ilam Church from the Italian Gardens. A white lady wanders between these two sites.

slightly right on a broad grassy track across next field, keeping straight ahead to an iron gate. (Ignore gate to the right). Go over the stile by the gate then follow wall on the right until you reach a gateway **in the wall.** At this point, turn left at 45° to the top left corner and a footpath sign.

5. Go through the gateway and then bear left to footpath sign and stile in the wall. Go through stile and to the right on a well defined path. Stay on this path, which follows the contours high above the Dove Valley for ¾ mile, giving superb views of the valley below. On reaching a lane (Larkstone Lane) go straight up one field with wall on the left. Cross stile into next field and bear right at 45° to a point midway down wall on the right. Cross three more fields in same direction to the road. Turn right and then left up the road to the pub, Ye Olde Royal Oak, in Wetton.

6. Coming out of the pub turn left and then left again through the churchyard to the road. Turn left and then, at the next road, go left over the stile by **sign** to Thor's Cave (but not heading to Thor's Cave). Go to the right of the cottage, over the next stile and ahead on a paved track. Follow footpath sign at top and continue in same direction over four fields to a road (Carr Lane). Turn right and then, after a short distance, turn right through stile down field, to another road (Larkstone Lane). Turn right and stay on this lane as it bends left and right down to Weag's Bridge.

7. Cross the bridge and the road and go through stile on other side, bearing left and then straight up the field. On reaching the road, turn left and follow road round right-hand bend, up the hill, then through a gate stile on the left. Drop down field, go over the stile, and at bottom of hill, turn left over second stile and go down valley, firstly on a wide grassy area, passing a dew pond and then through a steep sided gully which eventually becomes a more open area. Ignore a seeming path to the right and keep ahead on this open area. Go through a gap in a broken wall. The path starts to drop down and you finally follow the path round to the right to a stile on to the Manifold Way.

If it is getting dark and the moon is out, look both ways before stepping on to the Manifold Way. A phantom white horse with its headless rider is said to gallop through the Manifold Valley on moonlit nights.

It is supposed to be the ghost of a pedlar, murdered by two men, who cut off his head and set his headless body back on his horse and drove it across the moors. One report described the phantom as an 'awful gory sight'.

8. Cross over and go into Old Soles Wood. The path climbs steadily up through the wood for about ½ mile and then continues straight ahead on a broad path. Go over a stile and, with a wall on your right, go straight ahead. Where the wall ends, continue straight ahead. Go past a dew pond, cross a tarmacked road and ahead across a cattle grid on to a stony track. Go ahead on this track past buildings (Slade House) then keeping straight ahead where the track bears to the left. Then ahead on a grassy path, through another iron gate, then bear left over wooden stile where main track goes to the right. Go straight ahead where the path opens out into the field with a fence on the left. At the end of the wall, turn left down field and then left again at the bottom, over a stile by an iron gate.

9. Go ahead on a well defined path for 1½ miles through Musden Wood. On reaching a road, turn left and then, at the end of some buildings, turn right along a fence and up to a stile. Continue up the next field and follow the wall on the left in the next (retracing your path of this morning). Bear slightly left down next field, to a stile halfway down the wall on the opposite side. Cross the corner of the following field and cross the last one to the footbridge. Turn right on a broad path and stay on it until you reach the Battle Stone. Then bear left up the hill on a path to Ilam Hall. Pass to the right of the hall, down steps, then turn left in front of it to main drive. Bear right on to path, passing to the left of church. (Or go left on to main drive to return to the car park). Go through kissing gate on to a narrow path back to the road in the centre of the village.

Walk 28
Ilam 2

Although this is a shortened version of Walk 27, it has its own added ghostly tales of a lost child and a headless woman. Starting from Ilam, a very pretty village with its Alpine style houses, this is an easy walk, through fields and on the tracks and lanes, with good views. It returns through Musden Wood, which is very attractive though inclined to be muddy.

Distance: 5½ miles.
Grade: A.
Parking: On the main street of Ilam or in the car park attached to Ilam Hall.
Map Ref: SK136508. Outdoor Leisure 24 White Peak Area.
Pub Stop: None.

Ilam Hall is haunted by a 'White Lady' who has the habit of waking up people who are staying in the Youth Hostel, so if this is your base for walking you may be in for a sleepless night! She is also seen wandering the corridors and between the Church and the Italian Garden.

A phantom coach and horses is also said to be seen turning around in one of the old courtyards. Phantom coaches are usually completely black and may be a carriage or an actual hearse. They are pulled by headless horses, with a driver with skeletal or grotesque features. They are often driven at a furious pace and are thought to be seen prior to a death in the family.

Route

1. From the centre of Ilam village, go up Orchard View, then turn left over a stile and ahead on a broad track through the park. Where the track turns

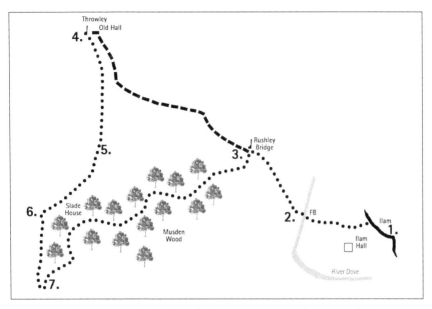

left, bear right to the left of the railed grassy area/pond. On reaching a stony track turn right down the hill. At the bottom, go ahead and turn left over a footbridge over the River Dove.

2. Cross the first field to the stile, then bear right, cutting across the corner of the next field. Continue in the same direction across next field on a broad grassy track. Go ahead parallel to the wall on your right, to another stile by a gate and cross next field. Then follow direction of finger post down next field to the stile to the right of the buildings. Go ahead by fence to lane.

3. On reaching the lane, turn left and then first right on to another lane. After a short distance, you pass a footpath to the left and a little further on, you pass a track to the left. Stay on the main lane for approximately one mile.

This lane, which leads to Throwley, is said to be haunted by a phantom coach known as the Cromwell Coach. In the daytime, only the sound of its wheels may be heard, but at night, its lights may be seen. Is this connected to the one seen turning round in Ilam Hall? It is said that anyone who gets in the way of such phantom coaches will be carried away to their doom!

Castern Hall.

However, if you have survived an encounter, you will eventually see the buildings of Throwley Hall ahead of you, with the ruin of the Old Hall in front.

The Old Hall dates back 300 years and was owned by the Cathcart family. As you travel towards the hall, you may meet a lost child, described as a golden haired boy, who may ask to be told the way home. If you enquire where he lives, he will point to Throwley but will then start to sob before disappearing before your eyes.

When you reach the ruin of what was once a magnificent building, note that on its west side, i.e. the left side when facing it, that there once stood a chapel. It is from here that a headless woman supposedly appears, who is said to terrify anyone passing by and followed one woman for a mile down the valley. However, you should be safe as she usually appears at midnight. Still, one never knows…

The ruins of Throwley Hall are haunted by a lost child and a headless woman.

4. Continue past the hall on the road for a short distance. Where the road bends to the right, you will reach a footpath sign for Calton, directing you to turn sharp left up the hill. The path (indistinct) climbs very steeply for a short distance and then continues parallel to the lane you have just travelled, heading for the left side of a wood to be seen ahead. As you approach the trees there is a wonderful view of Ilam and beyond. The path continues in the same direction, heading for a lone tree on the horizon (if it hasn't been blown down!) before bearing to the right, to what used to be the corner of the field (i.e. where a broken wall comes in from the left).

5. Go over a stile crossing a wall and then go ahead, contouring slightly left round the mound and then heading for a footpath sign to be seen in the wall ahead. Go over the stile in the wall, then follow the direction of the footpath sign, going diagonally across the field. On the far side of the field, head to the right of the gateway (i.e. not through it), going on to a broad path between a wall on the left and a stone structure on the right. Go ahead on this green lane and then over a stile by an iron gate. Continue in the same direction, keeping the wall on your left, then passing between two (wide

apart) walls, eventually reaching a gap stile. Go through a second gap stile to the right of an iron gate, on to a path between walls and then past a building to a lane, where you turn left. Pass the buildings and then keep straight ahead where the track bears to the left, going through a stile at the side of a wooden gate.

6. Then go ahead on a grassy path, through another iron gate, then bear left over wooden stile where main track goes to the right. Go straight ahead where the path opens out into the field with a fence on the left. At the end of the wall, turn left down field and then left again at the bottom, over a stile by an iron gate.

7. Go ahead on a well-defined path for 1½ miles through Musden Wood. On reaching a road, turn left, then at the end of some buildings, turn right along a fence and up to a stile. Continue up the next field and follow the wall on the left in the next (retracing your path of this morning). Bear slightly left down next field, to a stile halfway down the wall on the opposite side. Cross the corner of the following field and cross the last one to the footbridge. Turn right on a broad path and stay on it until you reach the Battle Stone. Then bear left up the hill on a path to Ilam Hall. Pass to the right of the hall, down steps, then turn left in front of it to main drive. Bear right on to path, passing to the left of the church. (Or go left on to main drive to return to the car park). Go through kissing gate on to a narrow path back to the road in the centre of the village.

Walk 29
Hulme End

A more energetic walk, with a number of hills (some steep), which climbs up to the village of Wetton, giving superb views over to Dovedale. It then takes in Thor's Cave and continues to the attractive Wetton Mill, ending with a splendid panoramic view of the Manifold Valley and surrounding countryside.

A Bronze Age copper mine, a folly and the ghost of a Roman soldier add even more interest to a superb walk.

Distance: 9 miles.
Grade: C.
Parking: Pay-and-display public car park at Hulme End. Take the B5054 from Hartington. Hulme End is reached after about 2 miles.
Map Ref: SK103594. Outdoor Leisure 24 White Peak Area.
Pub Stop: Ye Olde Royal Oak, Wetton.

Hulme End was the terminus of the former Leek and Manifold Light Railway which opened in 1904 and closed after only 30 years in 1934, later converted by Staffordshire Council to a bridleway from Hulme End to Waterhouses.

The name 'hulme' means an island or watermeadow, so this was a hamlet at the end of the watermeadow. Following a period of rain you may find that it still is when you cross the first field.

Route

1. Go out of the rear of the car park (i.e. opposite side to entrance) on to the Manifold Way, a broad track. After about 100 yards, turn left over a stile, then bear right across the field to a stile and ahead to a footpath sign, where you turn left over a bridge to a road by West Side Mill.

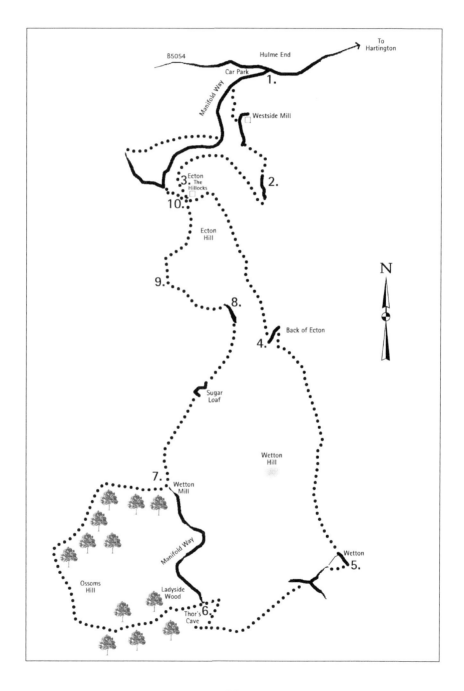

Turn right on the road. At a right-hand bend, turn left at the footpath sign, on to a paved road then cut across corner of field on the right, following direction of footpath sign to a stile 50 yards along the wall ahead. Go through stile and go diagonally right towards top corner. Go through stile in the wall to the right of house, then bear right down field to the left end of a protruding wall. Then go over the stile by stream and on to the road.

2. Turn left along road and then right at the footpath sign, following its direction parallel to driveway, past a small building, then turning sharp right to pass on the upper side of a broken wall above the houses, to a stile in the wall. Go straight across next two fields, through stile, then **immediately** left over another stile. With fence on your right, bear slightly left to a point 40 yards above the houses and go over the stile. Go on to a well marked path and keep straight ahead on this path until you reach some more houses. Go over the stile and down grassy slope.

N.B. In May the woods are full of wood anemones and a few bluebells and the hillside is ablaze with gorse.

The few houses below are all that remain of a settlement which thrived in the late 18th century due to the copper mining industry. About 300 people were employed in the mines, working day and night and earning one shilling (about 5p) for a six hour shift.

3. Turn left past the castle/folly and take a moment to examine this quaint structure.

Of all the places visited on the walks, this is one that looks as though it should have ghost but hasn't! Arthur Ratcliffe, who was Conservative MP for Leek, built this strange building called The Hillocks in 1935. There was originally a single-storey thatched cottage on the site. This was replaced by a two-storey dwelling with a flat concrete roof. As this leaked, another storey was built, together with a bridge, giving entrance from the nearby hillside and the copper spire, which was taken from a derelict chapel, was added. Mr Ratcliffe was renowned for his lack of attendance in the House of Commons. Perhaps he spent his time adding bits to his 'Folly'!

Go through the archway and over the stile to the left. Then go straight up the hill with a wall on your left. Continue climbing steeply up the hill, ignoring paths off to the right, until you reach a stone building on your left. Whilst you recover your breath, here is some interesting information about Ecton Hill and Ecton Mine which is to your right.

Deep Ecton Copper Mine went down to a depth of 1,380 feet from the summit. The mines in this area were not only some of the deepest in England but also the driest. This fact plus the quality of the ore made the mines extremely profitable for the Duke of Devonshire.

In 1998 a Bronze Age copper mine was discovered in Ecton Hill. An antler tool found inside, radio carbon dated the mine at nearly 4,000 years old, making it one of the earliest mines discovered in Britain. The ore would have been rare in those days and would therefore have been used to manufacture prestigious bronze objects, such as daggers and axes rather than everyday objects.

Now turn right along the wall – with the fence on your left (not through the gate). At the corner of the field, go ahead through the stile and on to a broad path with the remains of a wall on your right-hand side. There are excellent views at this point.

Keep straight ahead, crossing a field with a wall on your left. Go through stile and across next field to the stile in the top right-hand corner (i.e. not gateway) and straight ahead between walls and continuing on a broad path with a wall on the right. Go through gate on to lane and turn left. At junction, turn left and then turn right, just before house at the footpath sign.

4. Turn left at the next footpath sign and head diagonally across the field to the right-hand corner. Go over the stile and then bear right, before crossing the small stream on your left. Go to the left of the fenced group of trees on path and go up rise.

Go ahead on a broad path. Wetton Hill is ahead on the right. Go across a broad grassy area then, joining a wall on your right, go ahead over a stile. In next field, bear left to the stile two-thirds of way along fence on far side.

Thor's Cave, named after the Norse God of Thunder and haunted by a Roman soldier.

Go over the stile and ahead up the hill. Go over two fields and then ahead through gateway on to a broad lane to the right of reservoir.

Go down the lane to the road into the village of Wetton, which is at an altitude of about 1,000 feet. Turn left down the road to Ye Olde Royal Oak, an attractive oak-beamed pub.

5. Coming out of the pub, turn left and then left again through the Churchyard to the road. Turn left on road. Go past the road to Grindon and the Manifold Valley and go down the lane to the left marked 'To Thor's Cave'. The lane continues for ½ mile. You then come to a stile by a wooden gate and 30 yards further on, you will reach a stile over a wall at another sign for Thor's Cave. Go over this stile and turn left down the field. In the following field, continue by going down and then up to a stile on the far side. Go over the stile and turn right on a path round the hillside, which will eventually bring you to Thor's Cave.

Thor's Cave is thought to be named after the Norse god of thunder. It was excavated in 1864 under the direction of Samuel Carrington of Wetton and artefacts found in there, such as, flint arrowheads, bone combs, bronze bracelets and Roman pottery, suggest that the cave was in use throughout ancient times. A skeleton found there was thought to date from Neolithic times. It is said to be haunted by a Roman soldier, who is seen standing just inside the entrance.

After leaving the cave, drop down the steps to join a path and turn left, continuing down this path until you reach a bridge over the river.

6. If you wish to make this an easier walk, then turn right on the broad track in the Manifold Valley. Continue ahead on this track for about a mile, crossing a road, until you reach Wetton Mill, an 18th-century farm and mill now partly converted to a tea room. Your directions then continue at No 7. However, for a more scenic (but undulating) route, cross the Manifold Way and go over the stile opposite and up the path up the hill (marked Ladyside). Continue ahead on a clear path, which winds up through the woodland, emerging on a more open area, where the path turns left. On entering a field, follow a fence on your left. Continue up to a footpath sign where you go left. Go ahead on a clear path through trees. On reaching a more grassy open area, where the path divides, you should take the right-hand, uphill path, marked with an arrow post, 'To Wetton Mill'.

Go left over a small wooden bridge over a stream and ahead over the stile. Follow the direction of the finger post up a large field. On reaching a lane, cross straight over and over a stile on the far side. Then go diagonally right over the field to a stile by a wooden gate. Go down the fields through two wooden gates then moving to the left of a hedge, continue down to the bottom, where you meet a stream and a junction of paths. The sign at the bottom tells you that you have just descended Ossom's Hill.

Go over the bridge over the stream, following the sign to Wetton Mill and continue straight ahead with stream on your right for about ¾ mile until you reach a road. Turn right and then ahead over the bridge to Wetton Mill.

7. Turn right over a stone bridge then round track to the left and ahead to the buildings, following footpath sign marked 'Back of Ecton'. Go straight

The Ecton Folly: The Hillocks with its green spire.

through farmyard, then go through gate on to broad grassy track. Continue up this track going to the left of stony mound (named Sugarloaf). Go over the stile at top of rise then turn right to the stile in the wall. Turn left then immediately right along fence/wall for two fields. Then ahead again now with wall on the left. Continue until you reach a lane.

8. Turn left, then almost immediately left again at the footpath sign. Go over the stile over wall then up the field with wall on the right. Then turn right over the stile at next footpath sign and follow its direction across two fields. Cross to next stile, where a view opens up across the Manifold Valley to Butterton and the church spire of Grindon. Below in the valley is a charming bridge with reflections in River Manifold of bridge and trees.

9. After crossing the stile, drop down the field, but after 30 yards, turn right on a path going horizontally along hill, parallel to the valley below. Continue to a superb viewpoint over the Manifold Way looking towards Hulme End. Then drop down on a track, which is in line with the green spire of the Hillocks and then contours the hill to the right. Where the paths divide, take the left, lower path, which will take you below the horseshoe of trees to be seen ahead.

Near Wetton Mill in the Manifold Valley.

10. On reaching the buildings, go left over a stile, then right under arch. Go down the track to the road. Turn right then left and, if weary, go immediately right on to the Manifold Way. Stay on this track for about a mile back to the car park.

For a more attractive alternative, instead of turning on to the Manifold Way, go straight ahead up the hill (yes, another hill!) until you reach a footpath sign on the right. Turn right here and follow a clear path through trees and bushes for ½ mile until it eventually drops down to the Manifold Way. Turn left down to the car park.

Walk 30
Hollinsclough

A more strenuous 8-mile walk in superb scenery. It has a headless woman, an ancient packhorse trail and the magical Washgate Bridge, as the walk circles the spectacular Chrome Hill (pronounced Croom) before climbing it later in the walk. The wonderful views from the top make it well worth the effort.

Distance: 8 miles
Grade: C/D. Should not be attempted in bad weather.
Parking: In the village of Hollinsclough, 2 miles north-west of Longnor. There is limited parking at the side of the road, adjacent to the telephone box.
Map Ref: SK065665. Outdoor Leisure 24 White Peak Area.
Pub Stop: The Quiet Woman, Earl Sterndale.

When facing the telephone box, Chrome Hill is the rather large mound across the valley. Chrome Hill and its companion to the east, Parkhouse Hill, are fossilised coral reefs, formed over 350 million years ago as reef knoll mounds around a tropical lagoon. The reefs were more resistant to erosion than the surrounding limestone.

Route

1. Go up the narrow track, almost opposite the telephone box. After some buildings, turn left on a stony path. This path climbs steadily and then levels out. When you reach some buildings on the right go ahead on a tarmacked road. On reaching another building on the left, go ahead over a stile into a field. Cross four fields to reach the road.

   2. Cross the road and go down the lane on the opposite side, continuing

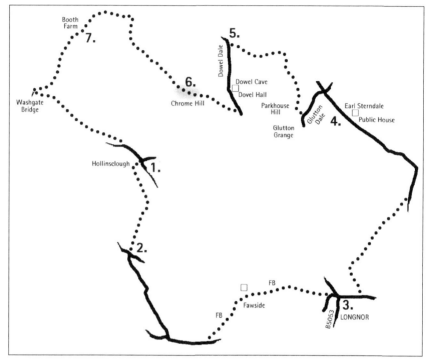

until you reach a main road. Turn left and then as the road starts to climb, go left on to a footpath. Follow direction of arrow down field, crossing footbridge and up to buildings (Fawside). Go through gate and to the right on a paved track, continuing past a barn on the left. Then bear right over a stile on to a footpath. It is pleasant place for a coffee stop. Continue on the footpath and after a second stile, go over two fields down to a double stile. Then climb up a third field and bear right following arrow on post, up to a stile in a wall. Continue through three more fields to a broad track where you turn right. On joining a road, go straight ahead to reach the centre of Longnor and crossroads.

3. Go straight over crossroads, passing the Market Hall on the left. Note the table of tolls listed on it which makes interesting reading. Continue straight ahead past the Cheshire Cheese pub until you reach the end of the houses where, just before the 'no limit' sign, you turn left up Dove Ridge.

Bear right opposite the house at the footpath sign on to a stony track. On reaching a small barn, go left and then right following a footpath sign. The route continues on a broad grassy path as it crosses the Upper Dove Valley. There are good views of Chrome Hill and Parkhouse Hill to the left. The path eventually reaches a lane where you continue ahead to a road. Turn left and continue climbing up the hill and into Earl Sterndale and the pub, The Quiet Woman.

Earl Sterndale Church was the only one in Derbyshire destroyed in World War Two. It was hit by stray incendiaries possibly intended for an explosives' dump in a quarry near Buxton. The church was restored in 1952.

The Quiet Woman pub is said to be haunted by the headless ghost of a woman, a former nagging wife, known as Chattering Charteris. The husband, driven to distraction by her nagging, lost control, cut off her head and then confessed his crime. The villagers not only forgave him but also had a whip-round to provide a headstone! It is an attractive old place with a warming fire in winter.

The Quiet Woman, Earl Sterndale, haunted by the ghost of a nagging wife who literally lost her head.

4. On leaving the pub, turn left and then left again at the crossroads (signposted Longnor) going down Glutton Dale.

This is an attractive steep-sided dale. The name refers, not to greedy locals, but to the largest member of the weasel family, the Wolverine, also known as a Glutton, a predator with a voracious appetite.

Where the road bends left, at a farm (Glutton Grange) go right across farmyard and on to stony track passing buildings on your left. Then, when you see a sign 'Bull in field,' go through the iron gate to the right of the sign. Go ahead on a broad grassy track with a wall on your left. On reaching a stony lane, turn left and then on reaching an iron gate on the right, go through it and over the stile and then ahead across the field following direction of footpath sign. Going over the next stile, the path drops steeply down, giving good views of Dowel Dale, eventually reaching the road.

5. Turn left and go down the road, passing Dowel Cave and Dowel Hall.

The Dowel Cave is situated in the hillside just before Dowel Hall. (No public access). It dates from Palaeolithic (Old Stone Age) times. The earliest known settlers of the White Peak used this cave.

A little further on, you will reach a stile on the right, with a notice of a concessionary path up Chrome Hill. Go over the stile and ascend the hill on a fairly clear path. It zig-zags its way to the summit, going almost straight up, crossing a stile halfway up. At the top, pause awhile to enjoy the superb panoramic views.

6. From the summit, continue along the ridge, on narrow paths, eventually dropping steeply down until you reach a stile. Go over the stile and to the right and on reaching a second stile, go right up side of fence, heading for an arrow post marker to be seen above. Continue to follow direction of arrow for the last bit of the climb, (the last bit I promise!). Bear left to next post marker and with wall on your right, continue ahead to next two stiles. Continue to a finger post and follow the arrow to Booth Farm. Go over the stile and ahead on a stony lane.

7. On reaching a tarmacked lane, turn left. Where the road forks go right, going past Booth Farm and continue ahead on the lower track. Continue down the lane, turning right on reaching two barns, up a slight rise and continuing down on the paved packhorse trail.

Where packhorse trains, which consisted of 40-50 horses, wore down the track and the rain washed it down also, as in this one, the ways became deeper and deeper and were known as hollow ways, which is often reflected in place names.

The track eventually leads down to Washgate Bridge.

Washgate Bridge, on a sunny day, is a magical spot. It is an original packhorse bridge only 4ft 6in wide, with parapets low enough so as not to catch the panniers of the horses and steeply humped to allow for floodwater. It is the nearest crossing to the source of the River Dove, which is at Dove Head Cottage on Axe Edge.

Cross the bridge over the River Dove and go to the left, crossing a second stream coming in from the right. Then continue parallel to the river on a path that is often muddy, all the way back to Hollinsclough. On reaching the road continue ahead to the parking spot.

John Lomas who was a pedlar from Flash, built the Methodist Chapel, at Hollinsclough (on the opposite corner of the junction). Many of the men from Flash supplemented their poor living from farming by peddling silk, mohair and twist buttons from Macclesfield to Flash. Locally they were called 'Fudge-Mounters' and they peddled their wares, as they travelled 'kippering and twanning', i.e. sleeping where they could in barns and begging for food.

Bibliography

Wayne Anthony *Haunted Derbyshire* Breedon Books Publishing Co Ltd, 1997.

David Bell *Derbyshire Ghosts and Legends* Countryside Books, 1993.

David Clarke *Ghosts and Legends of the Peak District* Jarrold Publishing, 1991.

Clarence Daniel *Derbyshire Traditions* Dalesman Publishing Co Ltd, 1975.

Clarence Daniel *Ghosts of Derbyshire* Galava Printing Co Ltd, 1973.

A. E. & E. M. Dodd *Roads and Trackways* Moorland Publishing Co Ltd, 1980.

David Hey *Packmen, Carriers and Packhorse Roads* Leicester University, 1980.

John N. Merrill *Halls and Castles of the Peak District and Derbyshire* J. N. M. Publications, 1988.

John N. Merrill *Winster: A Visitors Guide* J. N. M. Publications, 1985.

Lindsey Porter *The Peak District, its Secrets and Curiosities* Moorland Publishing Co Ltd, 1988.

Anton Rippon *Folktales and Legends of Derbyshire* Minimax Books Ltd, 1981.

Les Robson *Gazetteer of the White Peak* J. H. Hall & Sons, 1991.

R. I. Smith *Notable Derbyshire Houses* Derbyshire Countryside Ltd, 1972.

Index

ND - #0288 - 270225 - C0 - 210/148/12 - PB - 9781780911908 - Gloss Lamination